Contents

Sampler One

Garden Purse

Road to California Pillow

Sampler Two

Wild Rosebuds

Peony

Rocky Road to Kansas

Holiday Wreath

Christian Cross

Christian Cross

Garden Walk

Introduction

During the 1930's, most eggs were produced on rural farms with small flocks that scratched their way around the barnyard. The farmer's wife was usually responsible for caring for her chickens, and the money received from the sale of the eggs was hers. Surely, some fabric was purchased with this precious fund, and along with chicken feed sacks, came the quilts uniquely associated with the Depression years.

In *Egg Money Quilts,* there are two different styles of Samplers. Sampler One is constructed with 12" finished size blocks. Like days in the past, Sampler Two includes several different sizes of blocks. There is also a treasury of extra projects from the blocks created to emphasize their lasting versatility. Several quilt sizes are given, and you can always design your own by increasing or decreasing the number of blocks and borders.

It's fun to follow the *Egg Money* theme, but the Samplers don't need to be made from 1930's reproduction fabrics! These great traditional blocks can be made in any fabric. For variations on fabric and color themes as Batiks and 1860 reproduction fabrics, study the sample quilts throughout the book, and in the Student Gallery on pages 233-238.

During a time of hardship in America, there were still many things for which to be thankful. Life was simple, people neighborly, and quilts not only useful but also an extraordinary expression of imagination. Journey with me back to the times when milk was 14 cents a quart and bread nine cents a loaf. Enjoy the flavor of the "good old days" with snippets of life in America, recipes, and good old-fashioned fun.

Eleanor Burns

Quilts from Newspaper Patterns

Newspapers printed weekly quilt patterns in hopes that customers would buy a newspaper for something other than depressing bad news. Quilt blocks were all different sizes. Quilters often tried a pattern, just to see if they liked it well enough to make a whole quilt out of it. Consequently, they ended up with many different sizes of blocks. This sampler was made from multiple sizes of blocks in the 1930's.

These old newspaper patterns were a gift from Cleatis Hofer of Corpus Christi, Texas. Cleatis wrote, "These came from the newspaper, 'The Prospect News' in Doniphan, Missouri, which my mother subscribed to for many years. She passed the paper on to me, and the only thing of interest to me was the "Quilt of the Week."

Newspaper clippings were a gift from Cleatis Hofer.

Antique quilt from collection of Eleanor Burns

Fabric Selection

Reproduction Prints
To carry through the *Egg Money* theme, select a variety of 1930's reproduction prints. Avoid prints with excessive Background.

In addition, select various scales of prints, such as large scale, medium scale, small scale, and tone on tone. Plaids and polka dots also add charm to the quilt.

Multi-colored Prints
Select one multi-colored print that is your favorite. For interest, consider a large scale print. Use this fabric in the blocks, and, if you choose, as your widest border. Select a second multi-colored large scale print for an optional fussy cut in the center of Dresden Plate, or Road to California.

Refer to the dots of color on the selvage edge of the multi-colored print for guidance in selecting coordinating fabrics.

Background
Many quilts from the 1930's had solid colored flour and feed sacks for their background. For creating that look, select a quality 100% cotton, as Kona Cotton from Robert Kaufman Fabrics®. A favorite color that looks like muslin is Kona Natural.

Non-Woven Fusible Interfacing
Select non-woven light to medium weight fusible interfacing. One side of the interfacing is smooth in texture, while the other side has fusible dots. Do not confuse this interfacing with paper backed webbed fusing. Fusible interfacing is used to turn under raw edges of applique. The width is 22".

Sampler One – Yardage for Blocks

Yardage for Thirteen 12" Finished Size Blocks

Garden Walk

Dresden Plate

Christian Cross

Friendship

Turkey Tracks

Double
Wedding Ring

Rocky Road
to Kansas

Rosebuds

Peony

Grandmother's
Flower Garden

Road to California

Old Maid's Puzzle

Background 2⅓ yds

1930's Reproduction Prints
15 Different Fat Quarters
Fat quarters measure 18" x 20" – 22".

Multi-colored	2 fat quarters
Red	1 fat quarter
Pinks	2 fat quarters
Yellows	3 fat quarters
Blues	2 fat quarters
Purples	2 fat quarters
Greens	3 fat quarters

Muslin ¼ yd

Non-woven Fusible Interfacing 1½ yds
OR
Non-woven Fusible Interfacing ⅔ yd
   Mary's Flower Garden
     from Quiltsmart® – 1 Panel
   Double Wedding Ring
     from Quiltsmart® – 1 Panel

Additional Yardage
Turn to pages 10 and 11 for setting
selections plus additional yardage for
borders, backing, batting, and binding.

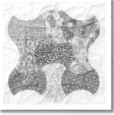

Double Ax Head

Bonus Block
Make all thirteen blocks, set the top
together with twelve, and use the last
one for the label.

Lap Setting

Pieced by Patricia Knoechel
Quilted by Judy Jackson
52" x 66"

Lattice 1 yd
(11) 2½" strips cut into
  (31) 2½" x 12½"

Cornerstones ¼ yd
(2) 2½" strips cut into
  (20) 2½" squares
or (20) 2½" scrappy squares

First Border ⅜ yd
(6) 2" strips

Second Border 1 yd
(6) 5" strips

Binding ⅔ yd
(7) 3" strips

Backing 3½ yds

Batting 60" x 72"

Rickrack 6 yds
(Optional)

Queen Setting

Frames for Blocks and Cornerstones
(12) ¼ yd pieces or
(12) fat quarters

Lattice 2 yds
(16) 4" strips cut into
    (31) 4" x 16½" strips

First Border 1 yd
(8) 3½" strips

Backing 9½ yds

Batting 96" x 114"

Straight Borders   or

Second Border 1¾ yds
(9) 6" strips

Third Border 2¾ yds
(Optional)
(10) 9" strips

Straight Binding 1 yd
(11) 3" strips

Scalloped Border

Scalloped Second Border 4½ yds
(10) 15" strips

Bias Binding 1 yd
(2) 16" strips cut into
    (20) 2" bias strips

Assembly-Line Cutting Sampler One Blocks

You can individually cut each block, or you can assembly-line cut all pieces for all blocks before you begin sewing for best use of time and fabric. Fabrics based on these charts have been equally distributed throughout the blocks. Before cutting, label a plastic quart size bag with name of each block. Cut all strips, and then cut strips into pieces. Place pieces in individual bags. Cutting instructions begin on page 26.

Background   2⅓ yds

❑ **(2) 13" strips cut into**
 ❑ (1) 13" square   Grandmother's Flower Garden
 ❑ (1) 13" square   Dresden Plate
 ❑ (1) 13" square   Double Wedding Ring
 ❑ (1) 13" square   Double Ax Head
 ❑ (1) 6" square   Rosebuds

❑ **(1) 7¼" strip cut into**
 ❑ (2) 7¼" squares   Old Maid's Puzzle
 ❑ (2) 7" squares   Rosebuds
 ❑ (1) 6½" square   Peony

❑ **(1) 5½" strip cut into**
 ❑ (2) 5½" squares   Old Maid's Puzzle
 ❑ (4) 5" squares   Road to California

❑ **(1) 5" strip cut into**
 ❑ (1) 5" x 16"   Garden Walk
 ❑ (4) 4½" squares   Peony

❑ **(1) 3¾" strip**   Rocky Road to Kansas

❑ **(2) 3½" strips cut into**
 ❑ (16) 3½" squares   Friendship

❑ **(1) 3" strip**   Turkey Tracks

❑ **(2) 3" strips cut into**
 ❑ (12) 3" x 2⅝"   Christian Cross
 ❑ (2) 3" squares   Christian Cross
 ❑ (2) 3" squares   Rosebuds

❑ **(1) 2½" strip cut into**
 ❑ (4) 2½" x 6"   Garden Walk

❑ **(1) 2" strip cut into**
 ❑ (16) 2" squares   Peony

Muslin   ¼ yd

❑ 7" x 14" strip   Rocky Road to Kansas

12

Non-Woven Fusible Interfacing   1½ yds

❏ **(1) 12" strip cut into**
   ❏ (1) 12" square   Double Wedding Ring

❏ **(1) 11" strip cut into**
   ❏ (1) 11" square   Flower Garden
   ❏ (1) 7" square   Flower Garden

❏ **(2) 5½" strips cut into**
   ❏ (4) 5½" squares   Old Maid's Puzzle
   ❏ (1) 5½" square   Dresden Plate
   ❏ (1) 5" square   Double Ax Head
   ❏ (1) 3½" x 5"   Peony
   ❏ (1) 3" square   Flower Garden

❏ **(2) 5" strips cut into**
   ❏ (8) 5" squares   Double Ax Head

OR

Non-Woven Fusible Interfacing   ⅔ yd

❏ **(2) 5½" strips cut into**
   ❏ (4) 5½" squares   Old Maid's Puzzle
   ❏ (1) 5½" square   Dresden Plate
   ❏ (1) 5" square   Double Ax Head
   ❏ (1) 3½" x 5"   Peony

❏ **(2) 5" strips cut into**
   ❏ (8) 5" squares   Double Ax Head

Mary's Flower Garden from Quiltsmart® **1 Panel**

Double Wedding Ring from Quiltsmart® **1 Panel**

Red   One Fat Quarter

❏ **(1) 7¼" half strip cut into**
   ❏ (1) 7¼" square   Old Maid's Puzzle
   ❏ (1) 7" square   Grandmother's Flower Garden
   ❏ (1) 5½" square   Old Maid's Puzzle

❏ **(1) 6" half strip cut into**
   ❏ (3) 6" squares   Peony

❏ (1) 2" x 15"   Peony
❏ (1) 2" x 9"   Peony

First Pink — One Fat Quarter

- ❏ **(1) 6" half strip cut into**
  - ❏ (1) 6" square — Rosebuds
  - ❏ (1) 5" square — Double Ax Head
  - ❏ (1) 4" square — Rocky Road to Kansas

- ❏ (1) 3" x 20" — Turkey Tracks

First Yellow — One Fat Quarter

- ❏ **(1) 4½" half strip cut into**
  - ❏ (3) 4½" squares — Road to California

- ❏ **(1) 4" half strip cut into**
  - ❏ (2) 4" squares — Double Wedding Ring
  - ❏ (1) 3½" square — Road to California

- ❏ **(2) 3" half strips cut into**
  - ❏ (1) 3" x 20" — Turkey Tracks
  - ❏ (2) 3" x 6" — Garden Walk
  - ❏ (1) 3" square — Grandmother's Flower Garden

- ❏ **(1) 2½" half strip cut into**
  - ❏ (3) 2½" x 6" — Garden Walk

Second Yellow — One Fat Quarter

- ❏ **(1) 2⅝" half strip cut into**
  - ❏ (1) 2⅝" x 6⅞" — Christian Cross
  - ❏ (2) 2⅝" squares — Christian Cross

- ❏ (1) 5" square — Double Ax Head
- ❏ (4) 2½" squares — Friendship

First Blue — One Fat Quarter

- ❏ **(1) 11" strip cut into**
  - ❏ (1) 11" square — Grandmother's Flower Garden
  - ❏ (1) 7¼" square — Old Maid's Puzzle

- ❏ **(1) 6½" strip cut into**
  - ❏ (1) 5½" square — Old Maid's Puzzle
  - ❏ (2) 3¼" x 15" — Turkey Tracks

First Purple — One Fat Quarter

- ❏ **(1) 6" half strip cut into**
  - ❏ (3) 6" squares — Road to California

- ❏ **(1) 3" half strip cut into**
  - ❏ (2) 3" x 6" — Garden Walk

- ❏ **(1) 2½" half strip cut into**
  - ❏ (3) 2½" x 6" — Garden Walk

- ❏ (4) 2½" squares — Friendship

14

First Green · One Fat Quarter

❏ **(1) 6" half strip cut into**
    ❏ (1) 6" square   Peony
    ❏ (1) 5½" square   Dresden Plate
    ❏ (1) 4" square   Rocky Road to Kansas
    ❏ (1) 3½" x 5"   Peony

❏ (1) 2" x 9"   Peony
❏ (1) 1" x 11" bias   Peony
❏ (1) 1¼" x 12" bias   Peony

Second Green · One Fat Quarter

❏ **(3) 2⅝" half strips cut into**
    ❏ (6) 2⅝" x 4⅝"   Christian Cross
    ❏ (2) 2⅝" x 6⅞"   Christian Cross
    ❏ (2) 2⅝" squares   Christian Cross

❏ **(1) 5" half strip cut into**
    ❏ (1) 5" square   Double Ax Head
    ❏ (2) 5" squares   Rosebuds

Multi-colored for Fussy Cuts · (Optional) One Fat Quarter

    ❏ (1) 5½" square   Dresden Plate
    ❏ (1) 3½" square   Road to California

Six Fat Quarters

Stack six remaining fat quarters right side up and layer cut.

❏ (6) 2½" x 11" strips cut into
    ❏ (24) 2½" squares   Friendship
❏ (6) 4¼" x 9"   Dresden Plate (one is extra)
❏ (6) 3" x 10" strips   Double Wedding Ring
❏ (6) 7" squares   Rocky Road to Kansas
❏ (6) 5" squares   Double Ax Head

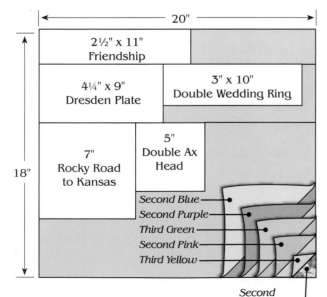

Sampler Two – Yardage for Blocks

Yardage for Twenty-Eight Various Size Blocks

One 24" Block

Peony

Two 18" Blocks

(1) Road to California

(1) Dresden Plate

Fourteen 12" Blocks

(2) Grandmother's Flower Garden

(1) Turkey Tracks

(3) Double Wedding Ring

(1) Rocky Road to Kansas

(1) Rosebuds

(1) Garden Walk

Four 9" Blocks

Christian Cross

Seven 6" Blocks

Friendship

(4) Old Maid's Puzzle

One 12" Bonus Block

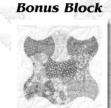

(1) Double Ax Head

Background 4½ yds

1930's Reproduction Prints
Five ½ yd pieces
- [ ] Pink   (1) ½ yd piece
- [ ] Greens   (2) ½ yd pieces
- [ ] Blue   (1) ½ yd piece
- [ ] Red   (1) ½ yd piece

Eleven Different ⅓ yd pieces
- [ ] Multi-colored   (2) ⅓ yd pieces
- [ ] Pinks   (2) ⅓ yd pieces
- [ ] Yellows   (3) ⅓ yd pieces
- [ ] Blue   (1) ⅓ yd piece
- [ ] Purples   (2) ⅓ yd pieces
- [ ] Green   (1) ⅓ yd piece

Muslin ¼ yd

Non-woven Fusible Interfacing 2⅓ yds
OR
Non-woven Fusible Interfacing 1⅓ yds
Mary's Flower Garden
     from Quiltsmart® – 1 Panel
Double Wedding Ring
     from Quiltsmart® – 1 Panel

Additional Yardage
Turn to pages 17 and 18 for setting selections plus additional yardage for borders, backing, batting, and binding.

Twin Setting

Pieced by Sue Bouchard
Quilted by Judy Jackson
63" x 84"

Border 1½ yds
(8) 6" strips

Binding ¾ yd
(8) 3" strips

Backing 6 yds

Batting 70" x 90"

Queen Setting

*Pieced by Teresa Varnes
Quilted by Judy Jackson
90" x 102"*

The colors used in this quilt match the designated colors in the assembly-line cutting charts.

Fabrics are from Moda, Inc®, Chanteclaire, and Clothworks.

First Border 1 yd
(8) 3½" strips

Backing 9½ yds

Batting 96" x 114"

**Rickrack (Optional)
8½ yds**

Straight Borders   **or**

Second Border 1¾ yds
(9) 6" strips

**Third Border   2¾ yds
(Optional)**
(10) 9" strips

Straight Binding 1 yd
(11) 3" strips

Scalloped Border

**Scalloped Second
Border 4 yds**
(9) 15" strips

**Bias Binding for
Scalloped Border 1 yd**
(2) 16" strips cut into
(20) 2" bias strips

Assembly-Line Cutting Sampler Two Blocks

You can individually cut each block, or you can assembly-line cut all pieces for all blocks before you begin sewing for best use of time and fabric. Fabrics based on these charts have been equally distributed throughout the blocks. Before cutting, label a plastic quart size bag with name of each block. Cut all strips, and then cut strips into pieces. Place pieces in individual bags. Cutting instructions begin on page 26.

Background   4½ yds

❑ (1) 19" square   Dresden Plate

❑ **(2) 13" strips cut into**
   ❑ (3) 13" squares   Double Wedding Ring
   ❑ (2) 13" squares   Grandmother's Flower Garden
   ❑ (1) 13" square   Double Ax Head

❑ **(1) 12½" strip cut into**
   ❑ (2) 12½" squares   Queen Setting
   ❑ (1) 12½" square   Peony

❑ **(1) 9½" strip cut into**
   ❑ (4) 9½" squares   Queen Setting

❑ **(1) 7½" strip cut into**
   ❑ (4) 7½" squares   Peony

❑ **(3) 7¼" strips cut into**
   ❑ (8) 7¼" squares   Old Maid's Puzzle
   ❑ (2) 7" squares   Rosebuds

❑ **(1) 6½" strip cut into**
   ❑ (4) 6½" squares   Road to California
   ❑ (1) 6½" square   Queen or Twin Setting

❑ **(1) 6" strip cut into**
   ❑ (1) 6" square   Rosebuds
   ❑ (2) 5½" squares   Old Maid's Puzzle
   ❑ (1) 5" x 16"   Garden Walk

❑ **(1) 5½" strip cut into**
   ❑ (6) 5½" squares   Old Maid's Puzzle

❑ **(1) 3¾" strip**   Rocky Road to Kansas

❑ **(4) 3½" strips cut into**
   ❑ (16) 3½" squares   Peony
   ❑ (28) 3½" squares   Friendship

❑ **(1) 3½" strip cut into**
   ❑ (1) 3½" x 24½"   Twin Setting
   ❑ (1) 3½" x 12½"   Twin Setting

❏ (1) 3" strip   Turkey Tracks

❏ **(1) 3" strip cut into**
   ❏ (8) 3" squares   Christian Cross
   ❏ (2) 3" squares   Rosebuds

❏ **(4) 2½" strips cut into**
   ❏ (6) 2½" half strips   Christian Cross
   ❏ (4) 2½" x 6"   Garden Walk

❏ **(2) 1¾" strips cut into**
   ❏ (4) 1¾" x 19"   Road to California

Muslin   ¼ yd

❏ (1) 7" x 14"   Rocky Road to Kansas

Non-woven Fusible Interfacing   2½ yds

❏ **(3) 12" strips cut into**
   ❏ (3) 12" squares   Double Wedding Ring
   ❏ (1) 7½" square   Dresden Plate
   ❏ (2) 7" squares   Grandmother's Flower Garden

❏ **(1) 11" strip cut into**
   ❏ (2) 11" squares   Grandmother's Flower Garden

❏ **(4) 5½" strips cut into**
   ❏ (16) 5½" squares   Old Maid's Puzzle

❏ **(3) 5" strips cut into**
   ❏ (9) 5" squares   Double Ax Head
   ❏ (1) 5" x 7½"   Peony
   ❏ (2) 3" squares   Grandmother's Flower Garden

Or

Non-woven Fusible Interfacing   1⅓ yds

❏ **(1) 7½" strip cut into**
   ❏ (1) 7½" square   Dresden Plate
   ❏ (1) 5" x 7½"   Peony
   ❏ (1) 5" square   Double Ax Head

❏ **(4) 5½" strips cut into**
   ❏ (16) 5½" squares   Old Maid's Puzzle

❏ **(2) 5" strips cut into**
   ❏ (8) 5" squares   Double Ax Head

Mary's Flower Garden from Quiltsmart® – 1 panel

Double Wedding Ring from Quiltsmart® – 1 panel

First Pink   ½ yd

❏ **(1) 7¼" strip cut into**
  ❏ (4) 7¼" squares   Old Maid's Puzzle
  ❏ (1) 7" square   Grandmother's Flower Garden

❏ **(1) 5½" strip cut into**
  ❏ (4) 5½" squares   Old Maid's Puzzle
  ❏ (4) 2½" squares   Friendship

First Green   ½ yd

❏ (1) 1¼" x 24" bias   Peony
❏ (1) 1⅛" x 20" bias   Peony
❏ (1) 9" square   Peony
❏ (1) 7½" square   Dresden Plate
❏ (1) 5" x 7½"   Peony
❏ (2) 5" squares   Rosebuds
❏ (1) 3½" x 15"   Peony
❏ (4) 2½" squares   Friendship

First Blue   ½ yd

❏ **(1) 5½" strip cut into**
  ❏ (4) 5½" squares   Old Maid's Puzzle
  ❏ (1) 5" square   Double Ax Head
  ❏ (1) 3" square   Grandmother's Flower Garden

❏ **(1) 11" strip cut into**
  ❏ (1) 11" square   Grandmother's Flower Garden
  ❏ (4) 7¼" squares   Old Maid's Puzzle
  ❏ (2) 3¼" x 15"   Turkey Tracks

5½" Old Maid's Puzzle	5½" Old Maid's Puzzle	5½" Old Maid's Puzzle	5½" Old Maid's Puzzle	5" Double Ax Head	3" Grma's FG
11" Grandmother's Flower Garden		7¼" Old Maid's Puzzle	7¼" Old Maid's Puzzle	7¼" Old Maid's Puzzle	7¼" Old Maid's Puzzle
		3¼" x15" Turkey Tracks		3¼" x15" Turkey Tracks	

Red   ½ yd

❏ **(1) 9" strip cut into**
  ❏ (3) 9" squares   Peony

❏ **(2) 3½" strips cut into**
  ❏ (3) 3½" x 15"   Peony
  ❏ (4) 2½" squares   Friendship

Second Green   ½ yd

- ❏ **(1) 5¼" strip cut into**
  - ❏ (1) 5¼" half strip   Christian Cross
  - ❏ (1) 4" square   Rocky Road to Kansas
  - ❏ (4) 2½" squares   Friendship

- ❏ **(2) 3¾" strips cut into**
  - ❏ (2) 3¾" half strips   Christian Cross
  - ❏ (2) 3¾" x 12"   Christian Cross

- ❏ (1) 2⅛" half strip   Christian Cross

First Yellow   ⅓ yd

- ❏ **(1) 5½" strip cut into**
  - ❏ (3) 5½" squares   Road to California
  - ❏ (1) 5" square   Double Ax Head
  - ❏ (1) 4½" square   Road to California

- ❏ **(1) 4" strip cut into**
  - ❏ (6) 4" squares   Double Wedding Ring
  - ❏ (2) 3" x 6"   Garden Walk

- ❏ **(1) 2½" strip cut into**
  - ❏ (3) 2½" x 6"   Garden Walk
  - ❏ (4) 2½" squares   Friendship

Second Yellow   ⅓ yd

- ❏ **(1) 3" strip cut into**
  - ❏ (1) 3" x 20"   Turkey Tracks
  - ❏ (1) 3" square   Grandmother's Flower Garden
  - ❏ (4) 2½" squares   Friendship

- ❏ (1) 7" square   Grandmother's Flower Garden
- ❏ (1) 5¼" x 12"   Christian Cross
- ❏ (1) 2⅛" half strip   Christian Cross

Second Pink   ⅓ yd

- ❏ (1) 11" square   Grandmother's Flower Garden
- ❏ (1) 6" square   Rosebuds
- ❏ (1) 4" square   Rocky Road to Kansas
- ❏ (1) 3" x 20"   Turkey Tracks

- ❏ (4) 2½" squares   Friendship

First Purple   ⅓ yd

- **(1) 7" strip cut into**
  - (3) 7" squares   Road to California
  - (1) 5" square   Double Ax Head

- **(1) 3" strip cut into**
  - (2) 3" x 6"   Garden Walk
  - (3) 2½" x 6"   Garden Walk
  - (4) 2½" squares   Friendship

Multi-colored for Fussy Cuts   (Optional) ⅓ yd

- (1) 7½" square   Dresden Plate
- (1) 4½" square   Road to California

Six ⅓ yd pieces for Multiple Blocks

Stack six remaining ⅓ yd pieces right side up and layer cut.

- **(1) 3" strip cut into**
  - (6) 3" x 30" strips   Double Wedding Ring
  - (24) 2½" squares   Friendship

- (6) 7" squares   Rocky Road to Kansas
- (6) 6" x 12"   Dresden Plate *(One is extra; eliminate one later)*
- (6) 5" squares   Double Ax Head

40"

(24) 2½" squares Friendship

3" x 30"
Double Wedding Ring

2½" 2½" 2½" 2½"

12"

7"
Rocky Road
to Kansas

6" x 12"
Dresden Plate

5"
Double
Ax Head

Second Blue
Second Purple
Third Green
Third Pink
Third Yellow
Multi-colored

Supplies

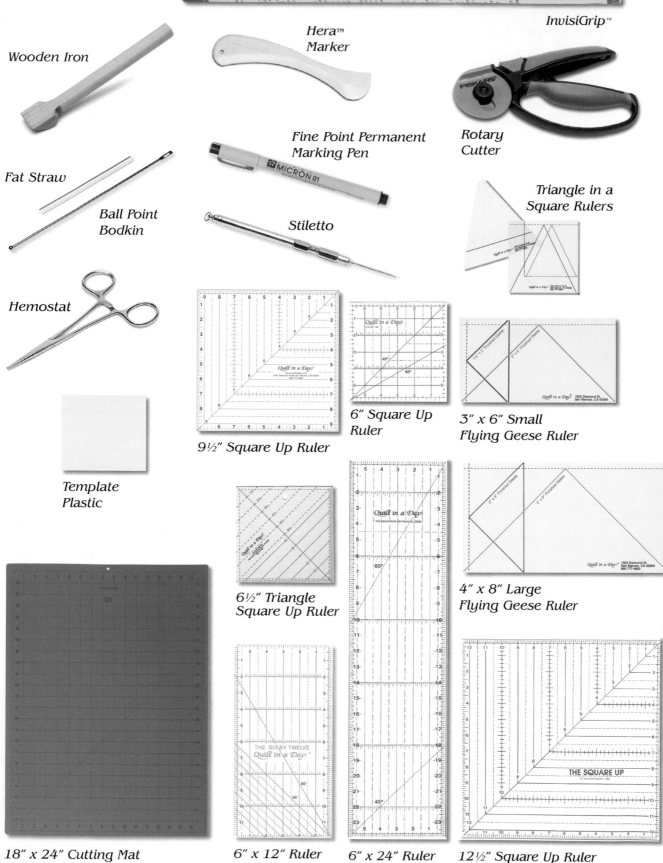

InvisiGrip™

Wooden Iron

Hera™ Marker

Fine Point Permanent Marking Pen

Rotary Cutter

Fat Straw

Ball Point Bodkin

Stiletto

Triangle in a Square Rulers

Hemostat

Template Plastic

9½" Square Up Ruler

6" Square Up Ruler

3" x 6" Small Flying Geese Ruler

6½" Triangle Square Up Ruler

4" x 8" Large Flying Geese Ruler

18" x 24" Cutting Mat

6" x 12" Ruler

6" x 24" Ruler

12½" Square Up Ruler

Sewing and Pressing Techniques

¼" Seam Allowance Test

¼" Foot

1. Place a ¼" foot on your sewing machine. Available for most sewing machines, a ¼" foot has a guide on it to help keep fabric from straying, giving perfect ¼" seams. Your patchwork is then consistently accurate.

   If you do not have a ¼" foot, adjust the needle position, change the presser foot, or feed the fabric under the presser foot to achieve the ¼". Complete the ¼" seam allowance test before starting your quilt.

2. Use a fine, sharp, #70/10 needle and a good quality of neutral shade polyester or cotton spun thread on your machine.

3. Cut three 1½" x 6" pieces.

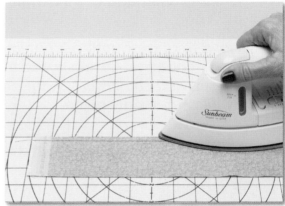

Set seam by pressing stitches.

4. Set machine at 15 stitches per inch, or 2.0 on computerized machines.

5. Sew two strips together lengthwise with what you think is a ¼" seam.

6. Place on pressing mat. Line up strip with lines on pressing mat. Set seam by pressing stitches.

7. Open and press against seam. Make sure no fold occurs at seam.

8. Sew third strip, and set seam. Open and press against seam.

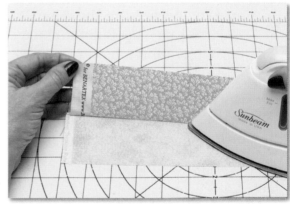

Open and press against seam.

9. Place sewn sample under a ruler and measure its width. It should measure exactly 3½". If sample measures smaller than 3½", seam is too large. If sample measures larger than 3½", seam is too small. Adjust seam and repeat if necessary.

   Use a consistent ¼" seam allowance throughout the construction of the quilt, unless directed otherwise.

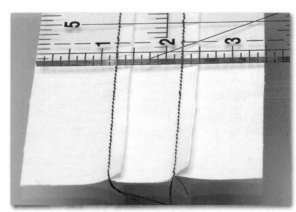

Sample should measure 3½".

Cutting Your Quilt

Put InvisiGrip™ on under side of all rulers.

Cutting Strips for Individual Blocks

1. Select designated fabric according to individual chart, and press. Place folded fabric on cutting mat.

2. Select ruler slightly longer than designated size. Best rulers to use for strips are the 6" x 24" Ruler and 6" x 12" Ruler. Straighten left edge.

3. Move ruler over until ruler lines are at newly cut edge. Carefully and accurately line up and cut strips selvage to selvage at measurements given.

Cutting Squares and Rectangles

1. Place single layer of fabric on cutting mat, right side up.

2. Select ruler slightly larger than designated size. Best rulers to use for cutting squares and rectangles are the 6" x 12", 6", 9½", and 12½" Square Up Rulers. Place ruler on left corner of fabric, lining up ruler with grain of fabric.

3. Rotary cut pieces on right side of ruler, and across top, slightly larger than designated size.

4. Turn piece and cut to exact size.

Cutting Bias Strips

1. Place single layer of fabric on mat, right side up.

2. Line up 45° line on 6" x 24" Ruler with left edge of fabric and cut. Corner piece of fabric can be used.

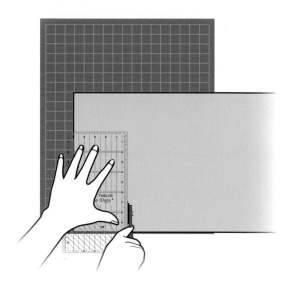

Fold

Selvages

Example shows 5" x 10" piece cut with 6" x 12" Ruler.

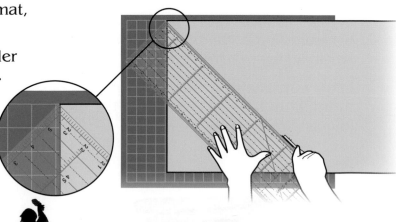

3. Move ruler over, and line designated bias strip width with diagonal edge. Cut bias strips.

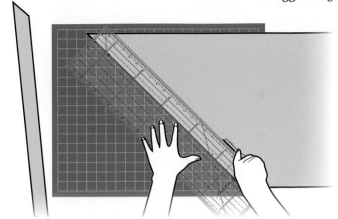

Assembly-line Cutting Blocks

1. Label a plastic quart size bag with name of each block.

2. Begin with Background. Place folded fabric on cutting mat. Straighten left edge.

3. Cut strip indicated width, selvage to selvage, with 6" x 24" Ruler. Use lines on ruler or mat for measurement.

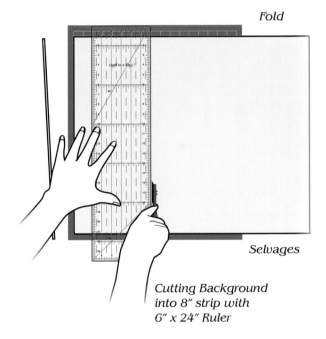

Fold

Selvages

Cutting Background into 8" strip with 6" x 24" Ruler

4. Turn strip and straighten left edge. Cut strip into indicated sizes of squares and rectangles.

5. Place each piece into appropriate block's bag.

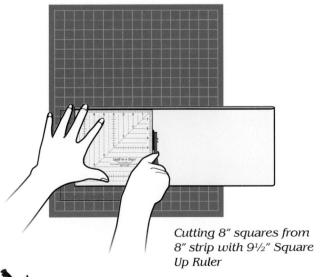

Cutting 8" squares from 8" strip with 9½" Square Up Ruler

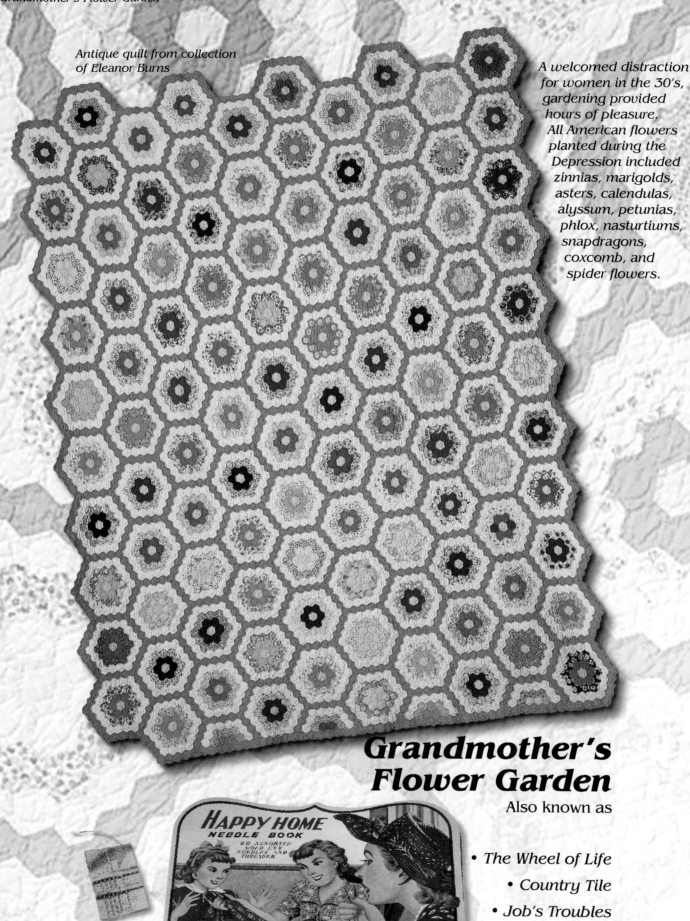

Antique quilt from collection of Eleanor Burns

A welcomed distraction for women in the 30's, gardening provided hours of pleasure. All American flowers planted during the Depression included zinnias, marigolds, asters, calendulas, alyssum, petunias, phlox, nasturtiums, snapdragons, coxcomb, and spider flowers.

Grandmother's Flower Garden

Also known as

- The Wheel of Life
- Country Tile
- Job's Troubles
- Honeycomb

HAPPY HOME
NEEDLE BOOK
60 ASSORTED GOLD EYE NEEDLES AND THREADER

Sampler One
One 12" Block
Finished Size

Background
(1) 13" square

Flower Center
(1) 3" square

Inner Petal
(1) 7" square

Outer Petal
(1) 11" square

Mary's Flower Garden
(1 panel from Quiltsmart®)
or Fusible Interfacing
(1) 3" square
(1) 7" square
(1) 11" square

100% Cotton Batting
(1) 2½" square
(1) 6½" square
(1) 10½" square

Sampler Two
Two 12" Blocks
Finished Size

Background
(2) 13" squares

Flower Centers
(2) 3" squares

Inner Petals
(2) 7" squares

Outer Petals
(2) 11" squares

Mary's Flower Garden
(1 panel from Quiltsmart®)
or Fusible Interfacing
(2) 3" squares
(2) 7" squares
(2) 11" squares

100% Cotton Batting
(2) 2½" squares
(2) 6½" squares
(2) 10½" squares

Supplies
❏ Permanent
  Marking Pen
❏ Point Turner
❏ Ball Point Bodkin
❏ Hemostat
❏ Thread Matching
  Three Flower Parts
❏ Invisible Thread
❏ Wooden Iron
  or Applique
  Pressing Sheet

Optional: Flower pieces printed on non-woven fusible interfacing by Quiltsmart® are available at Quilt in a Day and other quilt shops. No tracing is necessary – simply cut apart.

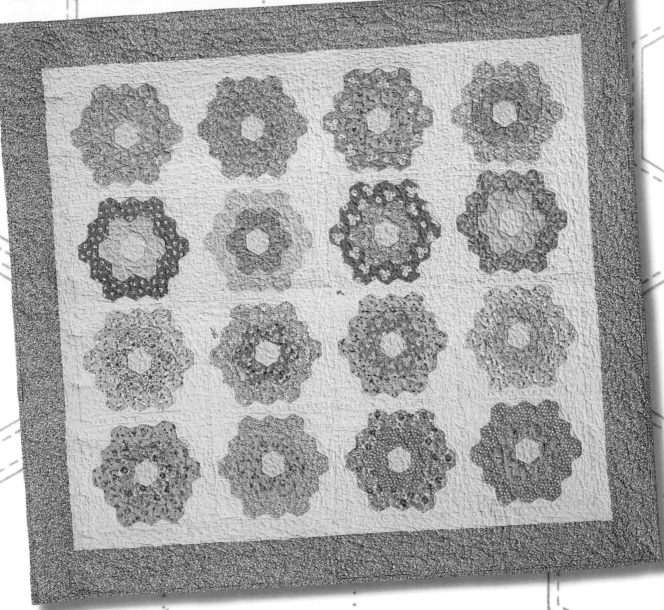

Pieced and Quilted by Anne Dease
50" x 56"

See *Mary's Flower Garden* from Quiltsmart® for complete yardage and sewing instructions for this quilt. If your local quilt shop does not carry these products, contact Quiltsmart®.

www.quiltsmart.com
email@quiltsmart.com

952.445.5737
888.446.5750 (Toll Free US & Canada)
Fax to 952.445.2136

Making Flowers

1. Find patterns on large pullout sheet in back of book.

2. Place appropriate size fusible interfacing on pattern, smooth size up.

3. Trace three flowers on interfacing with permanent marking pen, including inside lines.

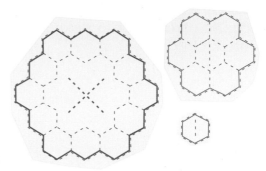

4. **Quiltsmart® Panel**: Rough cut around three flower pieces printed on fusible interfacing.

5. Place interfacing on fabric, with fabric right side up, and interfacing smooth side up. Pin.

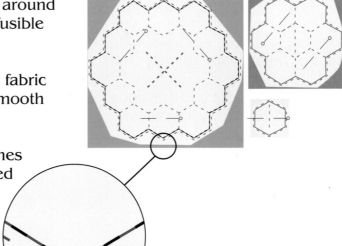

6. Sew on solid lines with 18 stitches per inch, or 1.8 on computerized machines. Use metal open toe presser foot. If available, lighten pressure on presser foot, and use needle down for pivoting with needle in fabric.

7. Cut ⅛" away from stitching.

8. Carefully clip inside points to stitches.

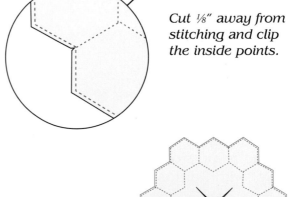

Cut ⅛" away from stitching and clip the inside points.

9. Slit interfacing, and turn each piece right side out.

10. Run point turner or ball point on bodkin around inside edge of each piece. Be careful not to poke a hole in interfacing.

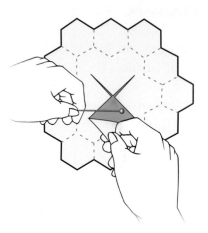

11. Pull out points with stiletto.

12. Press outside edges with wooden iron or press with steam iron on applique pressing sheet.

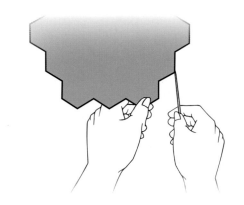

Stuffing Flowers (Optional)

1. Pin turned flower on appropriate size of batting. Cut batting into same size as flower.

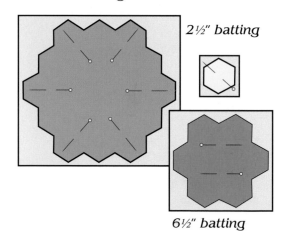

10½" batting

2½" batting

6½" batting

2. "Stuff" batting into slit of flower with hemostat. Manipulate batting to outside edges of flower with hemostat.

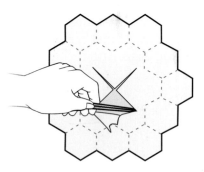

3. Place thread matching flower in bobbin and on top.

4. From wrong side of Outer and Inner petals, stitch on inside lines with 12 stitches per inch, or 3.0 stitch length on computerized machines. For speed, back track over previous stitching lines.

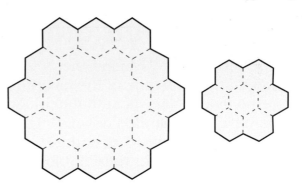

Finishing Flower

1. Press 13" Background square in half, and half again into quarters.

2. Center Outer Petal on Background square. Fuse in place with steam, first from right side, and then from wrong side.

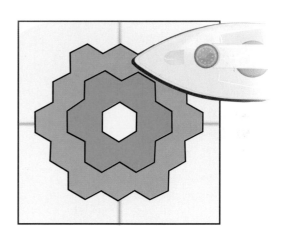

3. Center Inner Petal and Flower Center on top. Fuse in place.

4. Sew around each flower with matching thread or invisible thread. Tuck under exposed interfacing with stiletto before sewing over.
    Machine: *Use blind hem stitch.*
    Hand: *Use applique stitch.*

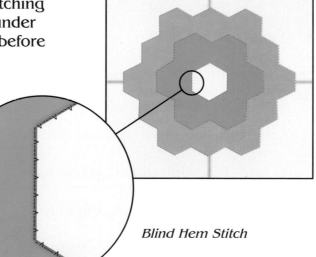

Blind Hem Stitch

5. Square block to 12½".
    Center 12½" Square Up Ruler on block, and trim on four sides.

Finishing Antique Blocks

During the 1930's, Grandmother's Flower Garden was one of the favorite patterns made. Many beautiful heirloom quilts have been handed down. But, judging from the stacks of antique Grandmother's Flower Garden blocks just waiting to be discovered, many were not completed! Quiltmakers apparently found it easy to sew three or four rings of hexagons together, but were stuck when they had to add the meandering path that wandered through the flowers.

If you are fortunate enough to find a stack of these colorful blocks at a flea market or antique store, turn them into a quilt using this same "fusible interfacing" method. Picture that long gone quilter smiling down on you!

1.   Check blocks. Repair or wash by hand if necessary.

2.   Press seams flat from wrong side.

3.   Place blocks right sides together to bumpy, fusible side of light weight fusible interfacing. Pin.

4.   Trim interfacing, leaving ½" around outside edges.

5.   Sew and turn, following directions on pages 31-33.

6.   Cut Background squares approximately 2" larger than flowers.

7.   Fuse in place, and sew around outside edges.

8.   Sew blocks together.

English Paper Piecing

These 1¼" paper hexagons and box covered with Japanese paper are remnants found in Gettysburg, Pennsylvania, from the 18th century. The hexagons were cut from a beautifully hand-written letter. They may have originated in England, and were used in a technique called English paper piecing.

The 18th century English quilter cut stiff paper into actual size hexagons, and cut pieces of cotton, silk, or wool ½" larger. The quilter then folded the edges of the fabric over the paper hexagon, and basted the fabric to the paper. Once basting was completed, the fabric hexagons were placed next to each other in a pattern, and slipstitched together. Once they were joined, the basting and paper was removed.

The hexagon pattern first appeared in women's magazines at the end of the first half of the 19th century. It maintained its popularity in the United States and was transformed slowly from the English model to the familiar Grandmother's Flower Garden of the 30's.

Bread Custard Pudding

1 1/2 cupfuls crumbled bread
1 tablesoonful butter
2/3 cupful sugar

1/2 teaspoonful vanilla
1 egg
3 cupfuls scalded milk

Combine the crumbs and milk, bring to boiling point, add the butter, and stir into the egg and sugar beaten light in the pudding dish. Flavour, surround the dish with hot water, and bake in a moderate oven — 350 degres F. — until a knife when inserted will come out clean — about forty-five minutes.

Apple Bread Pudding
Follow the directions in the preceding recipe, adding a cupful of grated apple to the mixture.

Ida Bailey Allen's Modern Cook Book, 2500 Delicious Recipes, Garden City Publishing Company, Inc., Garden City, New York, 1924

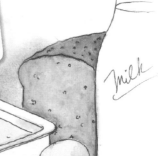

Grandmother's Garden Purse

Made by Eleanor Burns 10" x 15"

 Main Fabric ½ yd
Front and Back
(2) 10½" x 16½"
Handles
(2) 2½" x 30"

Bottom ⅜ yd
(1) 4½" x 16½"

Lining Fabric ½ yd
Pockets
(1) 16½" square
Lining
(2) 12" x 16½"

Rickrack 1⅛ yds
(1) 5" piece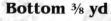

 Mary's Flower Garden
1 Panel from Quiltsmart®

or Non-woven Fusible Interfacing ¼ yd
(1) 6" x 11" for Outer Petal
(1) 7" square for Inner Petal

Flower Garden Patchwork
(1) 6" x 11" for Outer Petal
(1) 7" square for Inner Petal

Heavy Iron-on Interfacing 1 yd
(2) 10½" x 16½"
(1) 4½" x 16½"
(2) 1" x 30"

One Large 1" Button

36

Sewing Front and Back Together

1. Fuse iron-on interfacing to 4½" x 16½" Bottom and 10½" x 16½" Front and Back.

2. Sew Bottom between Front and Back.

3. Press seams toward Front and Back, and edgestitch.

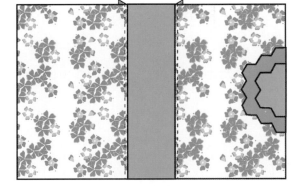

4. Trim fusible interfacing Outer Petal at 5½". Sew Outer Petal and Inner Petal with interfacing, trim, and turn. Refer to pages 31-33. Place Inner Petal on Outer Petal.

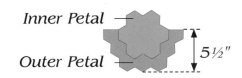

Inner Petal

Outer Petal

5½"

5. Find center of Grandmother's Flower Garden and center of purse Front. Position patch, and fuse in place. Trim to size.

6. Sew around outside edges of Grandmother's Flower Garden with invisible or matching thread and blind hem stitch.

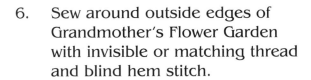

7. Place edge of rickrack with raw edge of Front. Sew through middle of rickrack with matching thread.

8. Sew rickrack to Back.

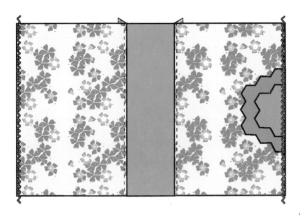

Making Pockets

1. Fold 16½" square in half wrong sides together.

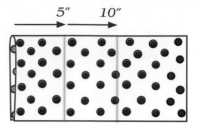

2. Draw lines at 5" and 10".

3. Place on top of 12" x 16½" back Lining, matching raw edges and sides.

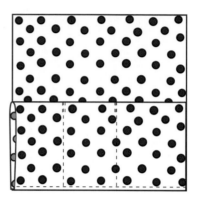

4. Sew on marked lines, backstitching at beginning for security.

5. Sew Pocket bottom to Lining.

Making Handles

1. Center and press iron-on interfacing on wrong side of 2½" x 30" Handles.

2. Fold lengthwise right sides together, and sew. Trim seam to ⅛". Turn right side out.

3. Turn seam to inside center, and press.

4. Mark 4¾" in from each side on front and back Lining.

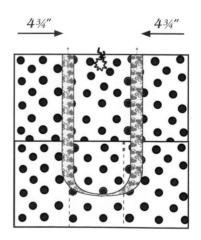

5. Pin Handles in place with seam next to right side of Lining fabric.

6. Fold 5" strip rickrack in half. Pin to center of back Lining.

7. Baste Handles and rickrack in place.

8. Pin and sew Pocket Lining to back Purse.

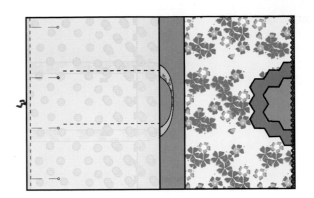

9. Pin and sew front Lining to front Purse.

10. Press seams toward Lining, and edgestitch.

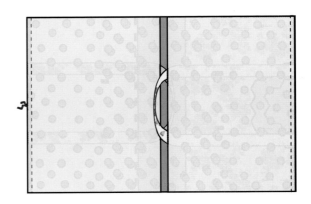

Finishing Purse

1. Fold Purse in half right sides together. Match and pin seams.

2. Sew three sides, leaving an 8" opening in middle of bottom.

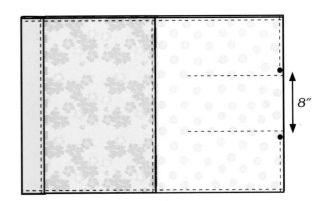

3. Flatten bottom, and pull out corners into triangle shapes. Mark a line 1¾" from end, and sew on line. Repeat on four corners.

4. Pull corners out through Lining opening and check from right side before trimming. Trim.

5. Turn right side out.

6. Hand sew opening shut. Tuck Lining into Purse.

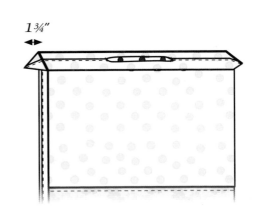

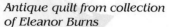

*Antique quilt from collection
of Eleanor Burns*

In the Great Depression,
the American dream
had become a
nightmare. Hope
for a better life was
California. Many Dust
Bowl farmers packed
their families into
cars, tied their few
possessions on the
back, and headed for
work in agricultural
fields and cities of
the West. It was the
largest migration in
American history!
After struggling
to make it to
California, many
found themselves
turned away at its
borders, or were
forced to follow
the crops for low
wages.

Road to California

Also known as

- *Flying Geese*
- *Wild Goose Chase*
- *Stepping Stones*
- *Crossroads*

Sampler One

One 12" Block
Finished Size

**Background
Corners**
(4) 5" squares

Medium Geese
(3) 4½" squares

Dark
(3) 6" squares

Center
Medium, Dark,
or Fussy Cut
(1) 3½" square

Sampler Two

One 18" Block
Finished Size

**Background
Corners**
(4) 6½" squares

Medium Geese
(3) 5½" squares

Dark
(3) 7" squares

Center
Medium, Dark,
or Fussy Cut
(1) 4½" square

Framing Border
Background or Print
(4) 1¾" x 19" strips

Supplies

❑ Permanent
Marking Pen

❑ 3" x 6" Flying
Geese Ruler for
Sampler One

❑ 4" x 8" Flying
Geese Ruler for
Sampler Two

❑ InvisiGRIP™

Making Geese

1. Place smaller square right sides together and centered on larger square.

   Sampler One
   4½" Medium Geese
   6" Dark

   Sampler Two
   5½" Medium Geese
   7" Dark

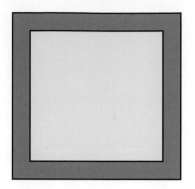

2. Place 6" x 24" ruler on squares so ruler touches through four corners. Draw diagonal line across squares. Pin.

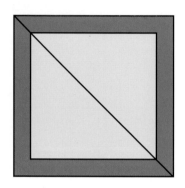

3. Sew exactly ¼" from drawn line. Use 15 stitches per inch or 2.0 on computerized machine. Assembly-line sew three sets of squares. Remove pins. Press to set seam.

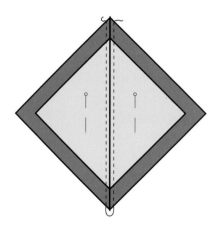

4. Cut on drawn line.

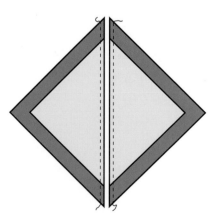

5. Place on pressing mat with large triangle on top. Press to set seam.

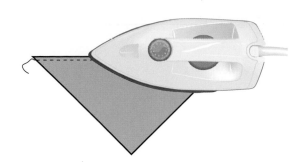

6. Open and press toward larger triangle. Check that there are no tucks.

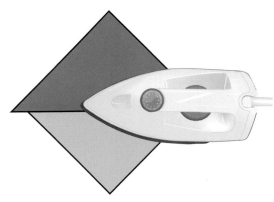

Press seam toward large triangle.

7. Place pieces right sides together so that opposite fabrics touch with dark matched to medium. Seams are parallel with each other.

8. Match up outside edges. Notice that there is a gap between seams. **The seams do not lock.**

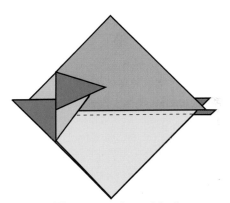

The seams do not lock.

9. Draw a diagonal line across seams. Pin. Sew ¼" from both sides of drawn line. Hold seams flat with stiletto so seams do not flip. Remove pins. Press to set seam.

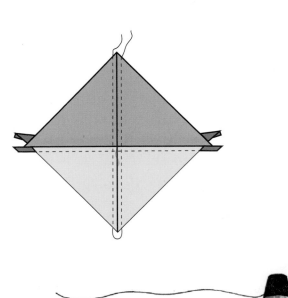

10. Cut on the drawn line.

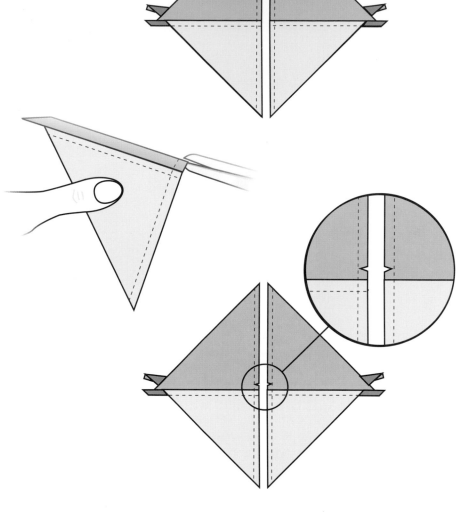

11. Fold in half and clip to the stitching. This allows the seam allowance to be pressed away from the medium geese triangle.

12. From right side, press into one medium triangle. Turn and press into second medium triangle.

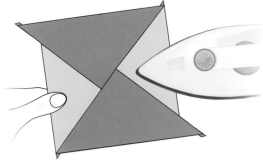

13. Turn over, and press on wrong side. At clipped seam, fabric is pressed in opposite directions.

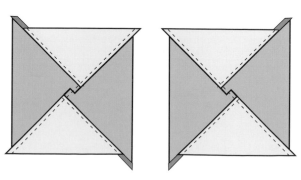

Squaring Up with Geese Ruler

1. Place InvisiGRIP™ on under side of ruler.

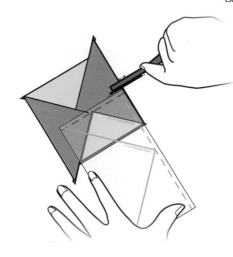

2. Line up ruler's red lines on 45° sewn lines. Line up dotted line with peak of triangle for ¼" seam allowance. Cut block in half to separate two patches.

Sampler One	Sampler Two
12" Block	18" Block
3" x 6" Flying Geese Ruler	4" x 8" Flying Geese Ruler
1½" x 3" Finished Geese	2" x 4" Finished Geese

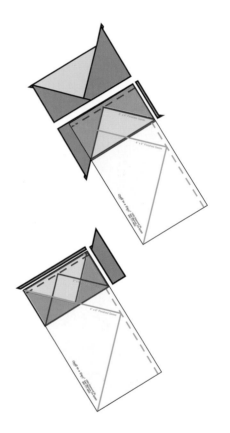

3. Trim off excess fabric on right. Hold ruler securely on fabric so it does not shift while cutting.

4. Turn patch around. Do not turn ruler. Line up green diagonal line on ruler with seam. Line up bottom of patch with red line. Trim off excess fabric on right and top.

5. Repeat with second half.

Sewing Geese Together

1. Divide Geese into three stacks with four in each.

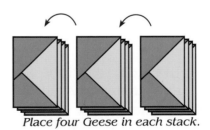

Place four Geese in each stack.

2. Assembly-line sew together.

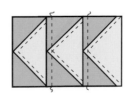

3. Press seams from base to point.

Sewing Block Together

1. Lay out Geese with Center and Corner Squares.

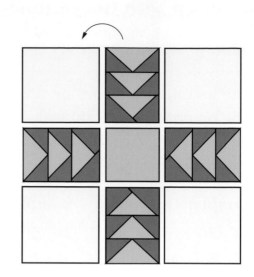

Sampler One	**Sampler Two**
12" Block	18" Block
3½" Center square	4½" Center square
5" Background Corners	6½" Background Corners

2. Flip center vertical row right sides together to left vertical row.

3. Assembly-line sew blocks together. Open.

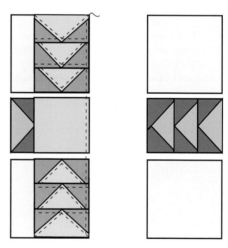

4. Flip right vertical row right sides together to center vertical row. Assembly-line sew blocks together. Open.

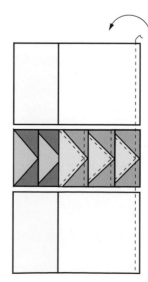

5. Set seams with Background on top. Open, and press seams away from Geese.

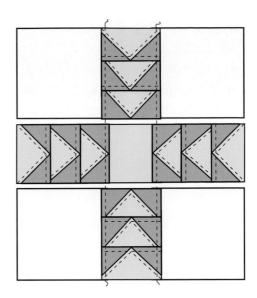

6. Turn block. Sew remaining rows together, matching seams. Open.

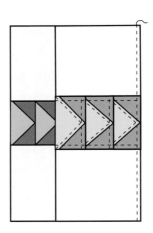

7. Press last seams away from center row.

8. Set aside 12½" block for Sampler One.

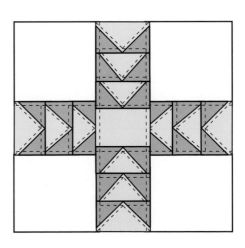

Adding Framing Border to 18" Block For Sampler Two

1. *Use Print or Background fabric.*
   Sew 1¾" strips to two opposite sides.

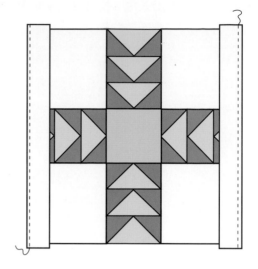

2. Set seams, open, and press toward
   Framing Border. Trim.

3. Sew 1¾" strips to remaining sides.

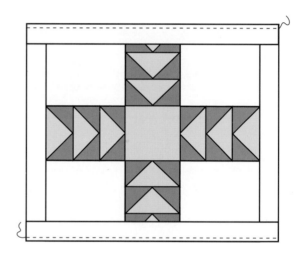

4. Set seams, open, and press toward
   Framing Border. Trim.

5. Square to 18½". Trim equally from
   four sides.

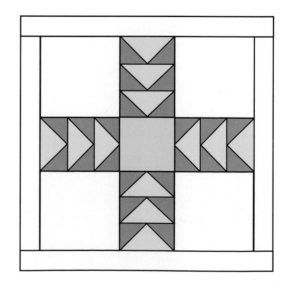

Road to California Pillow

Pieced by Eleanor Burns
19" Square

One 18" Block

Three Medium Geese ¼ yd each
(1) 5½" square from each

Three Dark ¼ yd each
(1) 7" square from each

Background Corners ¼ yd
(4) 6½" squares

Dark Center ¼ yd
(1) 4½" square

Framing Border ¼ yd
(4) 1¾" x 19" strips

Medium Ruffle ½ yd
(4) 3½" strips

Dark Ruffle ⅝ yd
(4) 4½" strips

Back ½ yd
(2) 13" x 19"

Pillow Form
(1) 20" form

Supplies

❏ Permanent Marking Pen

❏ 4" x 8" Flying Geese Ruler

❏ InvisiGRIP™

❏ Straight Pins

❏ 5 yds String

Making Block

1. Make Sampler Two 18" block following directions beginning on page 42.

2. Add Framing Border.

Making Ruffle

1. Sew four 3½" medium strips into one long strip. Sew four 4½" dark strips into one long strip.

2. Sew two long strips together lengthwise. Press seam toward dark.

3. Fold and press long strip in half lengthwise. On front side of Ruffle is a ½" dark border along folded side.

4. Seam short ends so strip is one continuous circle.

5. On back side of Ruffle, lay a string or crochet thread ¼" from raw edge. Zigzag over string, being careful not to catch string.

6. Divide circle into eight equal parts. Mark each part with a pin.

7. Pin Ruffle medium sides together to pillow front, matching middle and corner of each side.

8. Working on ⅛ of Ruffle at a time, draw up cord, and space gathers evenly. Pin and sew.

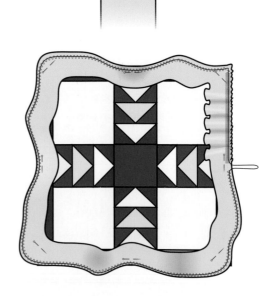

Finishing Pillow

1. Hem one 19" side on each Back piece.

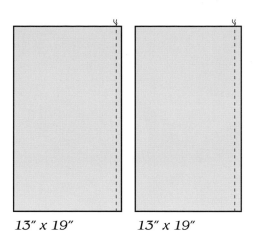

13" x 19"   13" x 19"

2. Overlap hemmed edges right sides together to pillow front.

3. Stitch around outside edge.

4. Turn right side out over 20" pillow form.

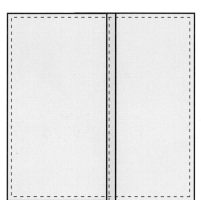

Burnt Sugar Cake

1 3/4 cupfuls white sugar
1/3 cup hot water
3 cupfuls sifted cake flour
3 teaspoonfuls baking powder
1/2 teaspoonful salt

3/4 cup butter
3 eggs
1 teaspoonful vanilla extract
2/3 cupful milk

Prepare burnt sugar by placing 1/2 cupful white sugar into a heavy skillet over medium high heat, stirring constantly with a wooden spoon as sugar melts. When it becomes very dark brown, remove from heat, add hot water very slowly and stir until dissolved. Set aside to cool.

Preheat oven to 350 degrees F. Line two 9 inch round baking pans with parchment paper. Sift the flour, baking powder and salt together three times. Cream the butter with the remaining 1 1/4 cupfuls white sugar until light and fluffy. Add the eggs, one at a time, beating thoroughly after each. Stir in the vanilla and the burnt sugar syrup mixture. Add the dry ingredients and milk alternately to the creamed mixture. Beat until smooth. Pour batter into the prepared pans. Bake at 350 degrees F for 25 to 30 minutes. Makes two 9" round layer cakes.

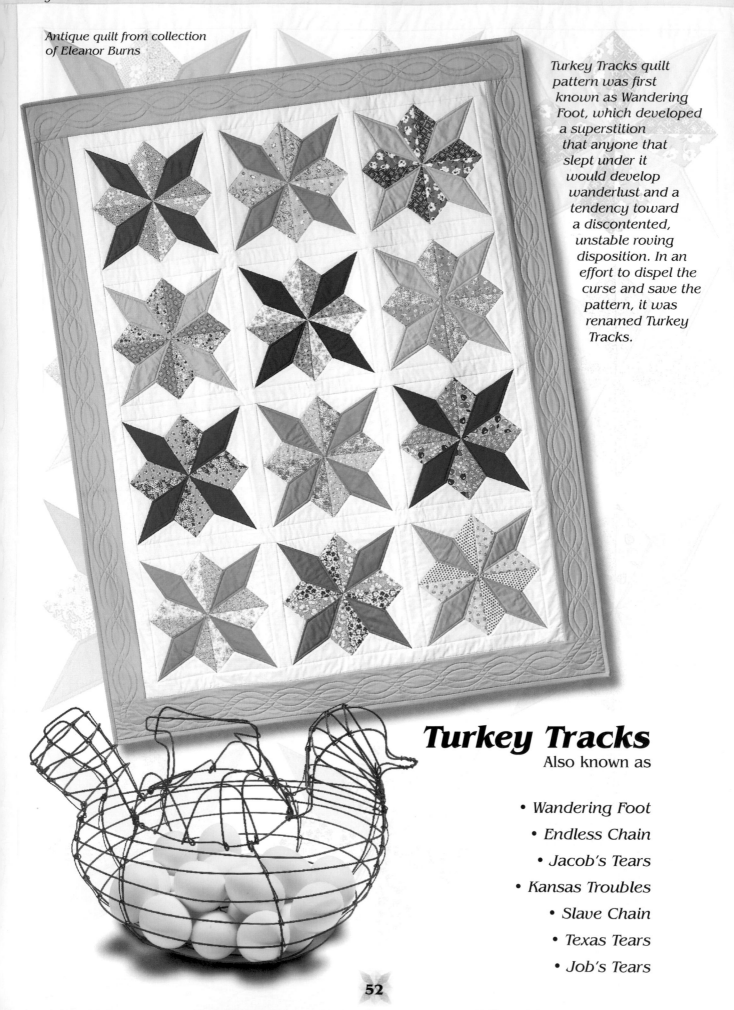

Antique quilt from collection
of Eleanor Burns

Turkey Tracks quilt pattern was first known as Wandering Foot, which developed a superstition that anyone that slept under it would develop wanderlust and a tendency toward a discontented, unstable roving disposition. In an effort to dispel the curse and save the pattern, it was renamed Turkey Tracks.

Turkey Tracks
Also known as

- *Wandering Foot*
- *Endless Chain*
- *Jacob's Tears*
- *Kansas Troubles*
- *Slave Chain*
- *Texas Tears*
- *Job's Tears*

Samplers One and Two
One 12" Block Finished Size
for each Sampler

Background
(1) 3" x 40" strip

Medium A
(1) 3" x 20" strip

Medium B
(1) 3" x 20" strip

Dark C
(2) 3¼" x 15" strips

Supplies

❏ Permanent
   Marking Pen

❏ Pencil or
   Disappearing Pen

❏ 6" x 12" Ruler

❏ Stiletto

❏ Pins

❏ Wooden Iron

Preparing Patterns

1. Find templates in back of book, and remove.

2. Push thumb tack or stiletto through dots and make a small hole.

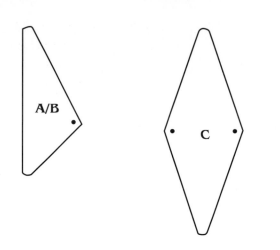

Cutting Pieces from A/B Template

1. Fold Medium A 3" x 20" strip in half lengthwise **right sides together**. Trace two sets of A/B template on strip.

   Carefully place A/B template so you can fit two.

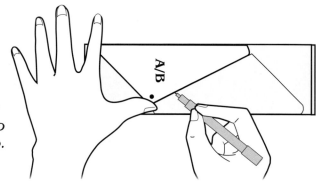

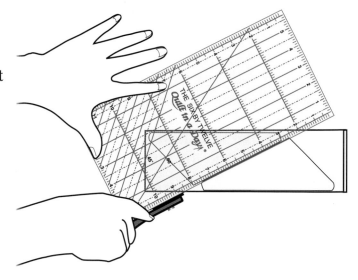

2. Cut dividing line between two pieces first, then cut other straight lines. Cut curved lines with scissors.

3. Lightly mark dot through template hole on wrong side of fabric with pencil or disappearing pen.

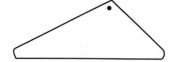

4. Fold Medium B 3" x 20" strip in half lengthwise **right sides together**. Trace two sets of A/B template on strip.

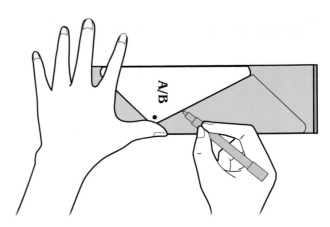

5. Cut out.

6. Lightly mark dot through hole on wrong side of fabric.

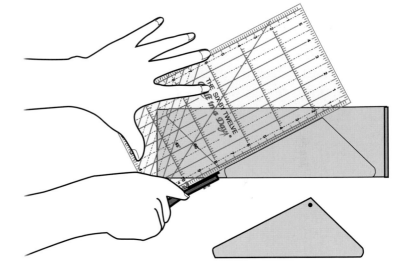

7. Fold Background 3" x 40" strip in half lengthwise **right sides together**.

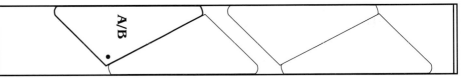

8. Trace two sets of A/B template on strip. Leave a 1" gap. Trace two more sets for a total of four.

9. Cut out. Lightly mark dot through hole on wrong side of fabric.

Cutting Pieces from C Template

1. Place C template on 3¼" x 15" strips **right sides together**.

2. Trace two C on strip.

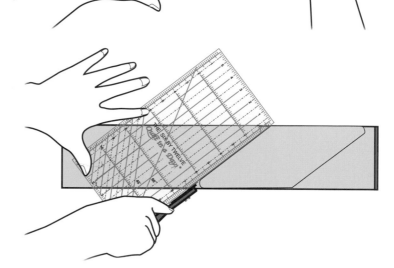

3. Cut straight lines with ruler and cutter. Cut curved lines with scissors. Lightly mark dots through template holes on wrong side of fabric.

Sewing A and C Pieces

1. Lay out A and C pieces right side up.

2. Flip right A onto C.

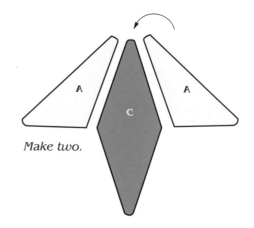

Make two.

3. Match and pin rounded ends. Pin through dots.

4. Use needle down position. Sew ¼" seam from rounded end and stop at dot. Lockstitch on dot.

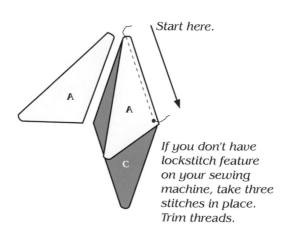

Start here.

If you don't have lockstitch feature on your sewing machine, take three stitches in place. Trim threads.

5. Open and fingerpress seam behind A.

6. Flip left A onto C. Match and pin rounded ends. Pin through dots.

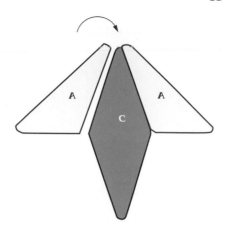

7. Turn. Lockstitch at dot, and sew ¼" seam from dot to rounded end.

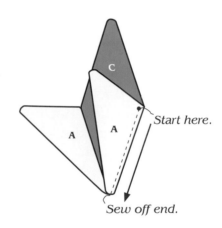

Start here.

Sew off end.

8. Open and fingerpress seam behind A.

9. Sew second set of Turkey Tracks with A.

Sewing B and C Pieces

1. Lay out B and C pieces for Turkey Tracks.

2. Sew two sets together same as A and C pieces.

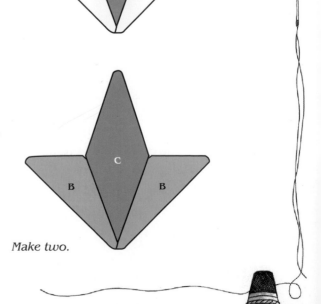

Make two.

Adding Background

1. Place Background with A/C Turkey Tracks.

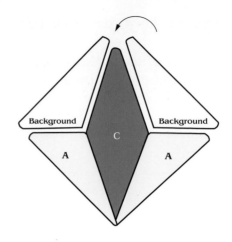

2. Fold A out of the way at dot.

3. Flip Background right sides together to C. Match Background and C rounded ends. Pin through Background dot. Sew from rounded end and stop at dot. Lockstitch on dot.

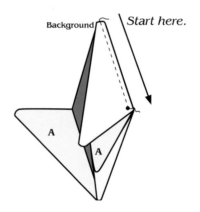

4. Complete seam by flipping Background to A, right sides together. Fold C out of the way. Match and pin rounded ends. Lock stitch on dot, and sew to rounded end.

5. Fingerpress seam behind Background.

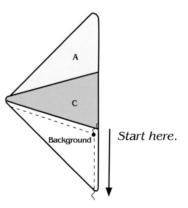

6. Repeat on second side. Fold A out of the way at dot.

7. Flip Background onto C. Match and pin rounded ends. Pin through dot. Lock stitch on dot, and sew from dot to rounded end.

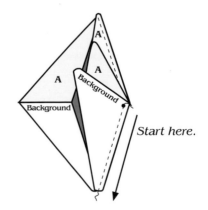

8. Fingerpress seams toward C.

9. Fold Background and A right sides together. Match rounded ends. Pin and sew to dot. Lockstitch on dot.

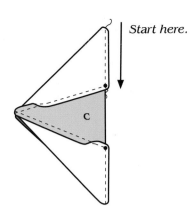

Start here.

10. Press seams away from C.

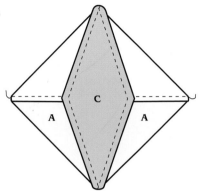

Back Side of Finished Block

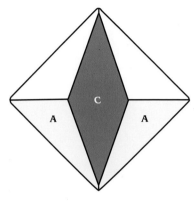

Front Side of Finished Block

11. Sew Background to B/C Turkey Tracks.

12. Press seams away from C.

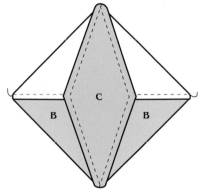

Back Side of Finished Block

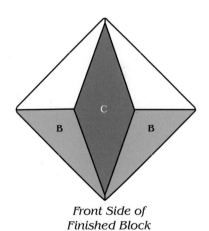

Front Side of Finished Block

13. Press. Place 6½" Triangle Square Up Ruler on patch. Sliver trim if necessary, leaving ¼" seam allowance.

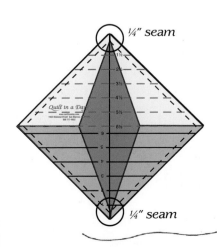

¼" seam

¼" seam

Sewing Block Together

1. Lay out four quarters in your selected variation.

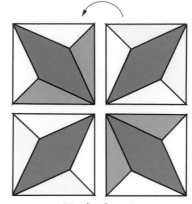

Variation 1
Seams lock together as pressed.

Variation 2
Seams lock together as pressed.

Variation 3
Repress A seams toward Background for locking seams.

2. Flip vertical row on right to vertical row on left, right sides together.

3. Match and pin seams. Assembly-line sew.

4. Turn, and sew remaining row. At connecting thread, push top seam up, and underneath seam down.

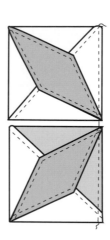

5. Clip connecting thread.

6. Fingerpress top vertical seam to right, and bottom vertical row to left. Center stitches open, creating a pinwheel.

7. Push pinwheel center flat.

8. Press seams.

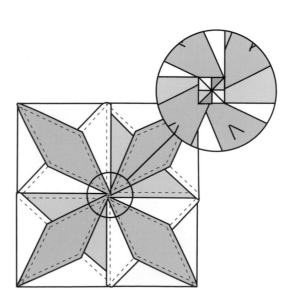

Turkey Tracks Sweatshirt

Patchwork

Medium A ⅛ yd
(1) 3" x 20"

Medium B ⅛ yd
(1) 3" x 20"

Dark C ⅛ yd
(1) 3¼" x 15"

Cuffs ⅛ yd
(2) 3¾" x 10½"

Bias Binding ½ yd
See page 26 for cutting bias strips.
Front
(6) 2" bias strips
Loop
(1) 1½" x 6" bias strip
Pocket Linings
(2) 6½" squares

Two 1" Buttons for Closure

Two ½" Buttons for Cuffs

Supplies

- ❏ Dressmaker Scissors
- ❏ Point Turner
- ❏ Stiletto
- ❏ 10" Piece of String
- ❏ Crewneck Sweatshirt

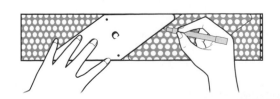

Making Two Patchwork Pockets

Follow directions beginning on page 54.

1. Fold Medium A 3" x 20" strip in half lengthwise right sides together. Trace two with A/B template.

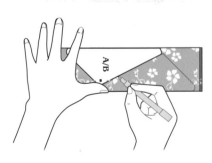

2. Repeat with Medium B 3" x 20" strip.

3. Cut out pieces.

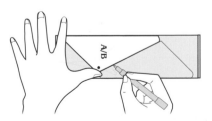

4. Trace C template on Dark C 3¼" x 15" strip.

5. Sew A to C.

6. Sew B to A/C.

7. Square to 6½".

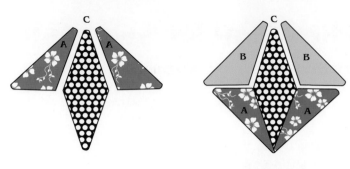

8. Place patchwork right sides together with 6½" Pocket Lining squares.

9. Sew around outside edge, leaving a 3" hole for turning.

10. Turn right side out through hole. Poke out points with point turner. Slip stitch opening shut.

Sewing Cuffs

1. Cut off ribbed sweatshirt cuff. Reinforce sweatshirt seam.

2. Fold 3¾" x 10½" Cuff strip right sides together lengthwise.

3. Sew two short ends together with ¼" seam.

4. Turn right side out. Pick out corners with stiletto and press. Baste raw edges together.

5. Fold sleeve flat. Measure Cuff against opening at end of sleeve. If opening is larger than Cuff, sew basting stitch around opening, and gather to size of Cuff.

6. Pin Cuff to opening, matching raw edges.

7. Sew around Cuff. Zigzag raw edges.

8. Overlap ends, and sew button through all layers.

Binding Front of Shirt

1. Cut off sweatshirt bottom ribbing.

2. Fold on center front, and cut on fold with scissors.

3. Make bias binding following directions beginning on page 231.

4. Sew bias binding around front, neckline, and bottom of shirt.

5. Pin Pockets in place on sweatshirt. Sew around three sides.

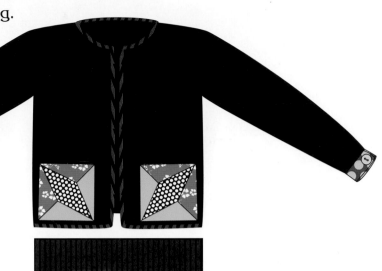

Making Bias Closure

1. Tie knot on end of 10" piece of string.

2. Lay string on right side of 1½" x 6" bias strip.

3. Fold bias strip in half lengthwise right sides together, and sew across top and down right side. Trim seam to ⅛".

4. Pull on string, and turn right side out. Press.

5. Make loop and fasten to neckline with button.

6. Sew second button to opposite side.

Pieced by Jeane Stellmack
Quilted by Judi Sample
51" x 63"

One of the first Civil Works Progress Projects built under the Works Progress Administration (WPA) was the Berkeley Rose Garden, considered by many to be the finest rose garden in northern California. The WPA was an agency created during the Depression to create jobs through government sponsored projects. The Rose Garden, conceived in 1933 and completed in 1937, has 3,000 rose bushes and 250 varieties of roses, along with breathtaking views of the San Francisco Bay and the Golden Gate Bridge.

Rosebuds

Also known as

- Bright Star
- Crow's Foot
- Hummingbird Comfort
- Maple Leaf

Yardage for this quilt is on page 73.

Samplers One and Two
One 12" Block Finished Size for each Sampler

Background
(1) 6" square
(2) 3" squares
(2) 7" squares

Rosebud
(1) 6" square

Leaf
(2) 5" squares

Supplies

❑ Permanent Marking Pen

❑ 6½" Triangle Square Up Ruler

❑ 6" x 12" Ruler

Making Rosebuds

1. Place 6" square Background right sides together to 6" square Rosebud.

2. Draw diagonal lines on wrong side of Background square.

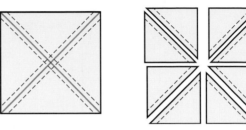

3. Sew ¼" from both sides of diagonal lines. Set seams.

4. Cut squares horizontally and vertically at 3". Cut on both diagonal lines.

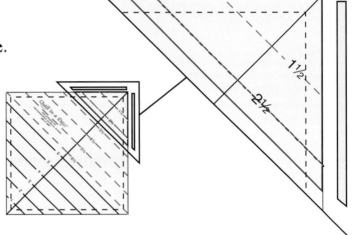

5. Place 2½" line on 6½" Triangle Square Up Ruler **on stitching line**.

6. Trim triangle to 2½".

7. Trim tips.

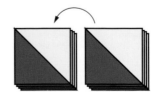

8. Lay trimmed triangle on pressing mat, dark side up. Lift corner, and press toward seam with tip of iron, pushing seams to dark triangle side.

9. Place four each in two stacks.

10. Assembly-line sew together. Do not press.

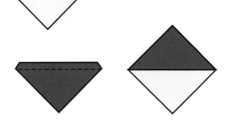

Move needle position to the right from a perfect ¼" seam to a scant ¼" seam.

11. Cut two 3" Background squares in half on one diagonal. Place with Rosebuds.

12. Assembly-line sew together.

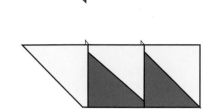

13. Press seams toward Background triangle. Trim tips.

14. Cut two 5" Leaf squares in half on one diagonal.

15. Place with Rosebuds. Assembly-line sew together.

16. Press seams toward Leaf.

17. Place 45° line on 6" x 12" Ruler across bottom edge of block.

18. Line up ruler's ¼" line with seam on right, and sliver trim not more than ⅛".

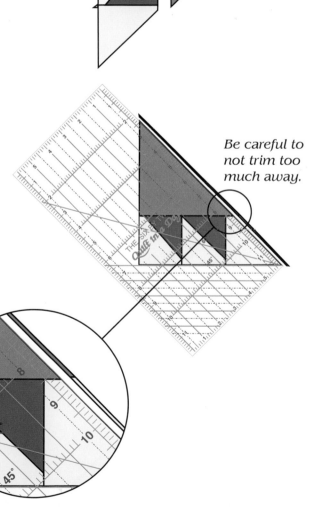

Be careful to not trim too much away.

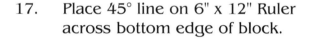

Finishing Block

1. Cut two 7" Background squares in half on one diagonal. Lay out with Rosebuds.

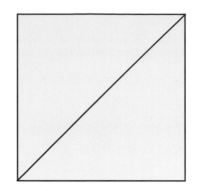

2. **Change back to ¼" seam.**

3. Place Rosebud triangle right sides together to Background triangle. Match 90° angles. Center Rosebud triangle on Background triangle.

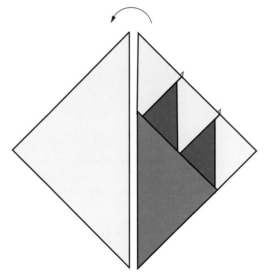

Change back to ¼" seam.

4. Assembly-line sew with Rosebud on top.

5. Press seams toward large Background triangle.

6. Place 6½" Triangle Square Up Ruler on block. Line up diagonal line on ruler with diagonal line on block. Sliver trim Background so block is 6½" square.

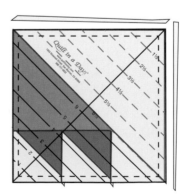

7. Lay out four blocks, and sew vertical row together, locking seams.

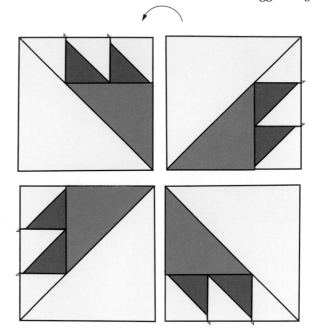

8. Sew remaining row. Lock seams, push top seam up, and underneath seam down.

9. Clip connecting thread.

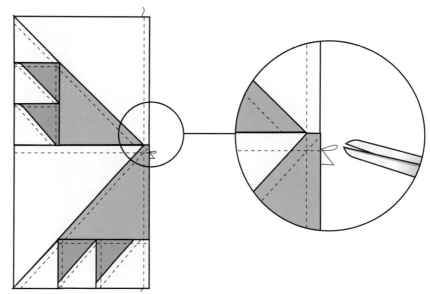

10. Place block wrong side up. Push top vertical seam to right, and bottom vertical seam to left. Center stitches pop open, forming a small pinwheel.

11. Flatten pinwheel with finger.

12. Press seams clockwise around pinwheel.

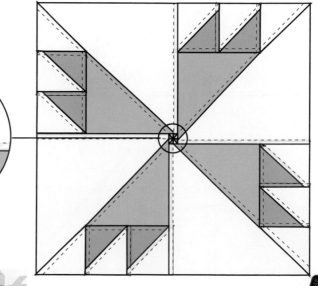

69

Rosebud Wallhanging

Background ⅓ yd
(2) 7" squares
(1) 6" square
(2) 3" squares
(2) 3" x 12½"

Red Rosebud ⅓ yd
(2) 6" squares
(3) 3" squares Prairie Points
(3) 2½" strips Binding

Pink Print ¼ yd
(2) 6" squares
(2) 3" squares Prairie Points
(1) 3¼" x 17" Top Border

Green Leaf ⅓ yd
(2) 5" squares
(1) 6" square
(3) 3" squares Prairie Points
(1) 4" x 17" Bottom Border

Buttons
(8) ½" for Prairie Points

Backing ¾ yd

Batting
24" x 30"

Pieced by Patricia Knoechel
Quilted by Teresa Varnes
17" x 23"

Making Wallhanging

1. Make one 12" Rosebud block following directions beginning on page 66.

2. Sew 3" x 12½" Background strips to top and bottom of block.

3. Set seams, open, and press toward Background.

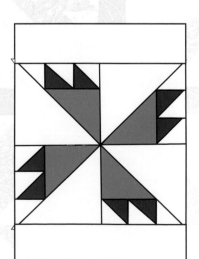

70

Making Side Borders

1. Place 6" square Pink right sides together to 6" square Rosebud.

2. Place 6" square Pink right sides together to 6" square Leaf.

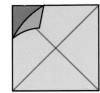

3. Following directions on page 66, make eight 2½" squares Pink/Rosebud, and eight 2½" squares Pink/Leaf.

4. Make two stacks of four each for both sets.

5. Assembly-line sew into four pairs each.

Place four in each stack.

6. Sew four pairs into strips of eight.

7. From wrong side, press seams to left.

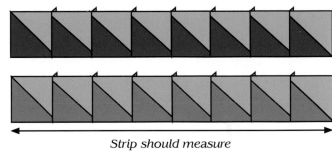

Strip should measure approximately 16½".

8. Place Pink/Leaf strip right sides together to right side of block. Line up center seam of strip with center seam on block. Background will extend on both ends. Pin, and sew.

9. Pin and sew Pink/Rosebud strip to left side of block.

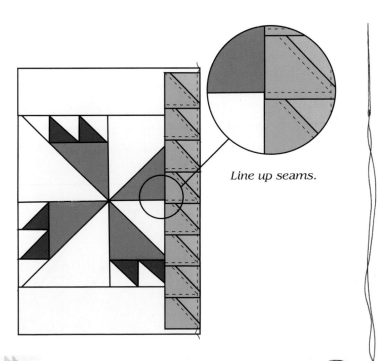

Line up seams.

10. Trim excess Background from top and bottom.

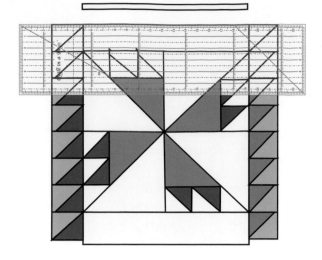

Adding Prairie Points

1. Fold eight 3" squares on one diagonal wrong sides together and press.

2. Fold in half again and press.

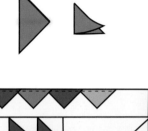

3. Arrange Prairie Points by matching raw edges with Background. Open first triangle. Slip next ones inside, overlapping as they are placed.

4. Pin in place, and baste with 12 stitches per inch or 3.0 on computerized machines with scant ¼" seam.

Adding Last Borders

1. Sew 3¼" x 17" strip Pink to top of Wallhanging. Set seam. Open, and press toward Pink. Trim if necessary.

2. Sew 4" x 17" strip Leaf to bottom of Wallhanging. Set seam. Open, and press toward Leaf. Trim.

3. Turn to *Layering Your Quilt*, page 224.

4. Sew buttons to Wallhanging through Prairie Points.

Wild Rosebuds

Pieced by Jeane Stallmack
Quilted by Judi Sample
51" x 63"

Background 1¾ yds
(5) 7" strips cut into
    (24) 7" squares
(2) 6" strips cut into
    (12) 6" squares
(2) 3" strips cut into
    (24) 3" squares

**Six Different Prints
¼ yd each**
(2) 6" squares from each
(4) 5" squares from each

Cornerstones
(20) Scrappy 2" squares

Lattice ¾ yd
(11) 2" strips cut into
    (31) 2" x 12½"

First Border ¼ yd
(6) 1¼" strips

**Second Border
and Binding 1½ yds**
(6) 4½" strips
(7) 3" strips

Backing 3½ yds

Batting 58" x 70"

1. Make two identical Rosebud blocks from each ¼ yd piece, using same fabrics for both Rosebud and Leaf.

2. Lay out blocks with 2" Lattice and Cornerstones.

3. Sew together following instructions for *Sampler One Lap*, beginning on page 202.

Old Maid's Puzzle

Antique quilts from collection of Eleanor Burns

On November 1, 1936, the first Sadie Hawkins Day was celebrated. Sadie Hawkins Day was named for a cartoon character developed by Al Capp for his Li'l Abner comic strip. All unmarried men in Dogpatch would get a ten minute head start before ugly Sadie and other unmarried women began running after them. The man each woman caught would end up in front of Marryin' Sam for a shotgun wedding.

Old Maid's Puzzle
Also known as

- Wanderer's Path in the Wilderness
- Wonder of the World
- Solomon's Puzzle
- Endless Trail
- Pumpkin Vine
- Drunkard's Path

This combination of patches can be set together eight different ways. See blocks on page 78. You can also design your own.

Sampler One

One 12" Block Finished Size

Non-woven Fusible Interfacing
(4) 5½" squares

Background
(2) 5½" squares
(2) 7¼" squares

Medium
(1) 5½" square
(1) 7¼" square

Dark
(1) 5½" square
(1) 7¼" square

Sampler Two

Four 12" Blocks Finished Size

Non-woven Fusible Interfacing
(16) 5½" squares

Background
(8) 5½" squares
(8) 7¼" squares

Medium
(4) 5½" squares
(4) 7¼" squares

Dark
(4) 5½" squares
(4) 7¼" squares

Supplies

- ❏ 6" x 12" Ruler
- ❏ 12½" Square Up Ruler
- ❏ Permanent Marking Pen
- ❏ Wooden Iron
- ❏ Ball Point Bodkin
- ❏ Fat Straw
- ❏ Applique Foot
- ❏ Invisible Thread

Optional: Use only one fabric with Background. Add Medium and Dark together for number of squares to cut.

Making Old Maid's Puzzle

1. Remove 4½" circle template from back of book.

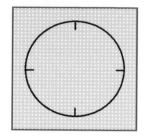

2. Center and trace circles on smooth side of 5½" squares of lightweight fusible interfacing. Mark lines at quarter marks.

Sampler One	**Sampler Two**
(4) 5½" squares	(16) 5½" squares
Fusible Interfacing	Fusible Interfacing

3. Place bumpy side of interfacing against right side of 5½" squares. Pin.

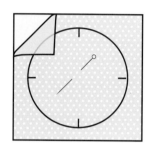 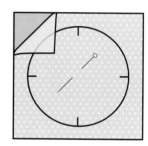 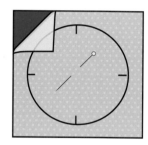

Sampler One	**Sampler Two**
(2) 5½" Background	(8) 5½" Background
(1) 5½" Medium	(4) 5½" Medium
(1) 5½" Dark	(4) 5½" Dark

4. Place metal open toe foot on sewing machine. If possible, lighten pressure on presser foot.

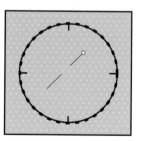

5. Sew on drawn line with 20 stitches to the inch or 1.8 on computerized machines. Overlap beginning and ending stitches.

6. Trim circles to ⅛". Cut a slit in middle of interfacing.

7. Turn circle right sides out with ball point bodkin and straw. Run bodkin around inside. Press with wooden iron.

See pages 140-141 for turning applique with ball point bodkin and straw.

8. Press 7¼" squares in fourths. Center circles on squares, matching up quarter marks.

Sampler One	**Sampler Two**
(2) 7¼" Background	(8) 7¼" Background
(1) 7¼" Medium	(4) 7¼" Medium Blue
(1) 7¼" Dark	(4) 7¼" Dark Red

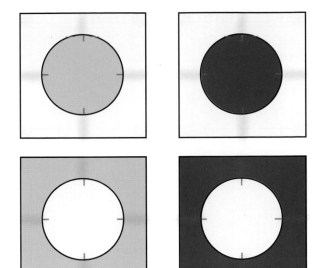

9. Steam press circles in place from right side and wrong side.

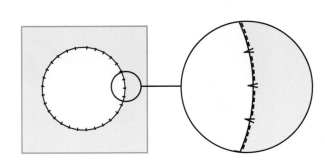

10. Blind hem stitch by machine with matching or invisible thread. Hand applique if you prefer.

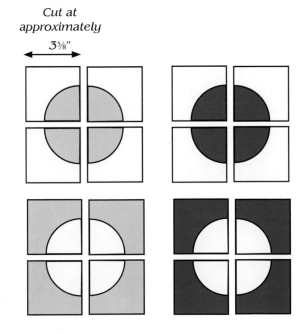

11. Cut squares in half on vertical and horizontal lines.

    Cut at approximately

    3⅝"

12. Turn patch to wrong side. Trim bottom layer of quarter circle ¼" from stitching line.

Sewing Block Together

Sampler One

1. Lay out one block.

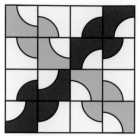

Old Maid's Puzzle

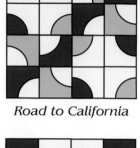

Road to California

Polka Dots

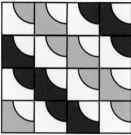

Love Ring

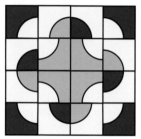

Mosaic

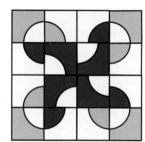

Diagonal Stripes

Rob Peter to Pay Paul

Fool's Puzzle

Sampler Two

Lay out four blocks.

Old Maid's Puzzle in optional two fabrics

2. Divide block into four parts.

3. Flip patches on right vertical row over patches on left vertical row. Assembly-line sew.

Illustrations are for Old Maid's Puzzle. Yours may be different.

4. Turn and flip row on right to row on left.

5. Push seam on top up and underneath seam down. Assembly-line sew.

6. At center seam, cut the first stitch with scissors. Remove the two or three straight stitches with a stiletto or seam ripper. Turn over and repeat on other side.

7. Place block wrong side up.

8. Open center seams and push flat to form a tiny four-patch.

9. Press seams clockwise around block.

10. Square up patches to 6½" square with 12½" Square-up Ruler. Trim equally on four sides.

Place 3¼" line on center seam.

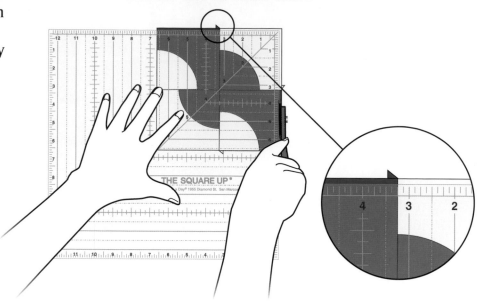

11. Lay out four quarters.

12. Flip right vertical row to left vertical row, and sew.

13. Open and sew remaining seam. Push seam on top up and underneath seam down.

14. At the center seam, cut the first stitch with scissors. Remove the two or three straight stitches with a stiletto or seam ripper. Turn over and repeat.

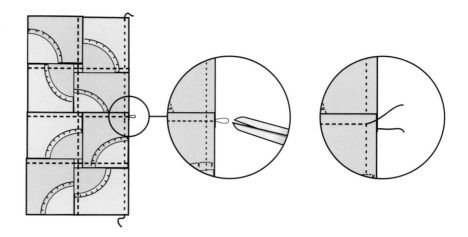

15. Open center seams and push flat to form a tiny four-patch.

16. Press seams clockwise around block.

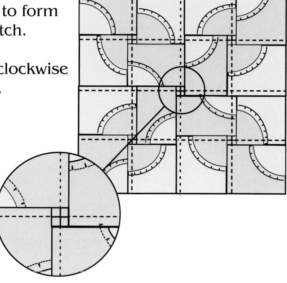
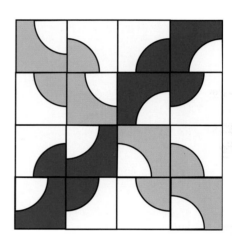

17. **Sampler Two:**
Sew four 12½" blocks into one 24½" block.

Yo-Yo
Table Doily

Center ⅛ yd
(1) 4½" circle

Inner Ring ¼ yd
(6) 4½" circles

Outer Ring ¼ yd
(12) 4½" circles

Supplies

❑ Permanent Marking Pen

❑ Hand Quilting Thread

❑ Hand Sewing Needle

❑ Thread Conditioner

❑ Thimble

Making Yo-yos

1. Find 4½" circle template from Old Maid's Puzzle in back of book and remove.

2. Trace 4½" circles on wrong side of fabric with permanent marking pen, and cut out.

3. Thread hand sewing needle with a double strand of matching thread, and knot. Pull thread through thread conditioner so thread doesn't tangle.

4. From wrong side, turn under raw edge ¼" and run a long gathering stitch near folded edge.

5. Turn right side out, gather tightly, flatten, and adjust gathers. Knot on front side, or push needle through center, and knot on back.

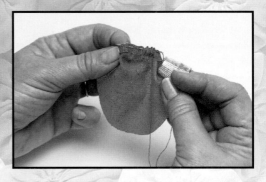

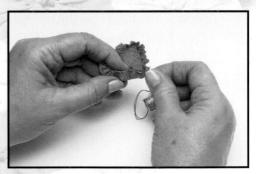

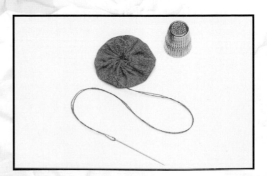

6. Set zigzag machine stitch width to 4.0 mm.
    Set stitch length to 0.

7. Place two yo-yos from inner ring side by side.
    With matching thread and open toe foot,
    machine zigzag two together.

8. Continure to sew six inner ring yo-yos together
    in a row.

9. Join two outside yo-yos into a circle.

10. Sew inner ring to center circle.

11. Sew twelve outer ring yo-yos
    together in a row.

12. Join two outside yo-yos into a circle.

13. Sew outer ring to inner ring.

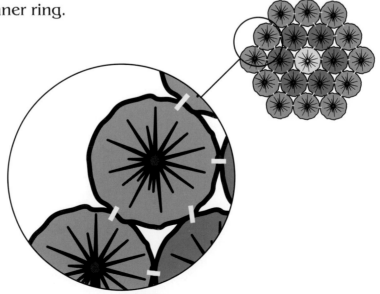

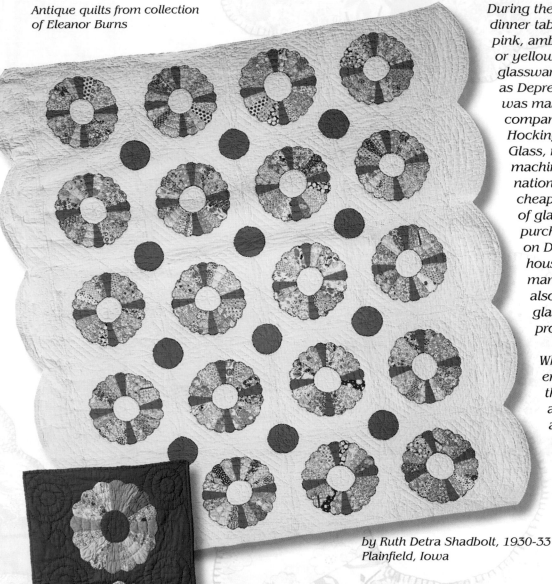

*Antique quilts from collection
of Eleanor Burns*

During the 1930's, many dinner tables were set with pink, amber, green, blue or yellow glassware. This glassware became known as Depression glass. It was mass produced from companies as Anchor-Hocking and Jeanette Glass, made totally by machine, distributed nationally and sold cheaply. Single pieces of glassware could be purchased for a nickel on Dish Nite at movie houses. Laundry soap manufacturers would also throw a piece of glassware into their product.

When the Depression ended, many people threw their glassware away, for they were a reminder of difficult times.

*by Ruth Detra Shadbolt, 1930-33
Plainfield, Iowa*

Dresden Plate
Also known as

- Aster
- Friendship Ring
- Friendship Daisy
- Sunflower

𝒯here are yardage charts and instructions for a 12" block, an 18" block, and five different sizes of quilts. Turn to pages 90-91 for quilt yardage.

Sampler One
One 12" Block
Finished Size

Background
(1) 13" square

Five Medium to Dark
(1) 4¼" x 9" from each

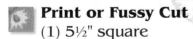

Print or Fussy Cut
(1) 5½" square

**Non-woven Fusible
Interfacing**
(1) 5½" square

Sampler Two
One 18" Block
Finished Size

Background
(1) 19" square

Five Medium to Dark
(1) 6" x 12" from each

Print or Fussy Cut
(1) 7½" square

**Non-woven Fusible
Interfacing**
(1) 7½" square

Supplies

❏ Stiletto
❏ 6" x 12" Ruler
❏ Applique Foot
❏ Permanent Marking Pen
❏ Invisible Thread
❏ Ball Point Bodkin
❏ Fat Straw
❏ Applique Pressing Sheet
❏ Pins

Cutting Wedges

1. Find wedge template in back of book, and remove.

2. Stack five fabrics wrong side up, with lightest on top.

3. Trace four wedges.

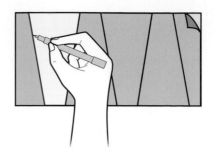

4. Layer cut wedges with 6" x 12" ruler.

5. Stack wedges right sides up.

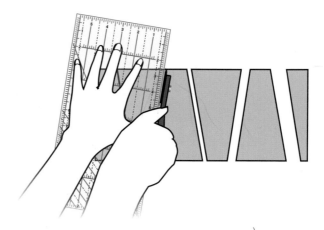

Sewing Wedges

1. Fold wedge in half lengthwise, right sides together.

2. Assembly-line sew ¼" seam from fold on wide top edge.

3. Clip apart in groups of five.

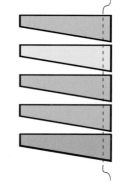

4. Trim seams to ⅛". Cut connecting threads.

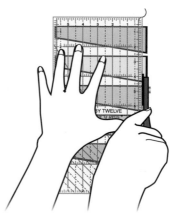

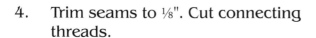

5. Turn right side out. Pick out point with stiletto.

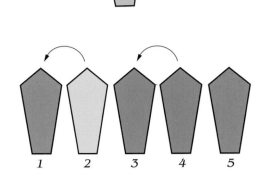

6. From wrong side, center seam on point, and press.

7. Stack five different wedges right side up in preferred color order. Place four wedges in each stack.

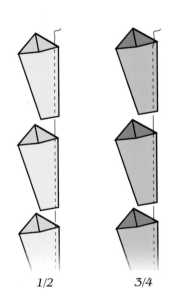

8. Assembly-line sew 1 and 2 into pairs, and 3 and 4 into pairs. Clip apart and open.

9. Assembly-line sew 1/2 and 3/4 together. Clip apart and open.

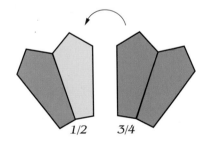

10. Sew 5 to 1/2/3/4. Clip apart.

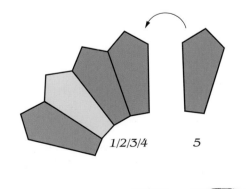

11. Sew quarters together into one circle.

12. Lay circle **flat** wrong side up on pressing mat. Fingerpress seams open. Carefully steam press without stretching fabric.

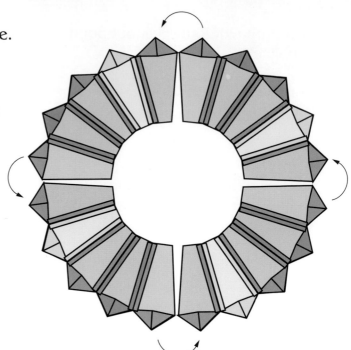

Making Circle

1. Remove circle template from back of book. Trace circle on smooth side of non-woven fusible interfacing square.

Sampler One	**Sampler Two**
12" Block	18" Block
4½" circle	6½" circle
5½" square	7½" square

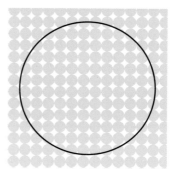

2. Place bumpy, fusible side of interfacing on right side of fabric.

Sampler One	**Sampler Two**
12" Block	18" Block
5½" square	7½" square

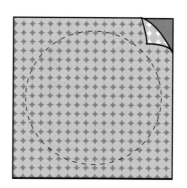

3. Sew on line with 18 stitches per inch, or 1.8 on computerized machines. *Overlap beginning and ending stitches.*

4. Trim ⅛" away from stitching.

5. Cut small slit in center of interfacing.

6. Turn right side out with straw and ball point bodkin.

7. Press outside edges with wooden iron or iron and applique pressing cloth.

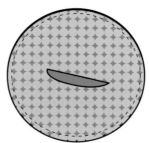

See pages 140-141 for turning applique with ball point bodkin and straw.

Finishing Dresden Plate

1. Press Background square in half, and half again into quarters.

2. Carefully center Dresden Plate on Background square, lining up seams with folds.

   For a balanced look, place dominant colored wedge in same position as purple.

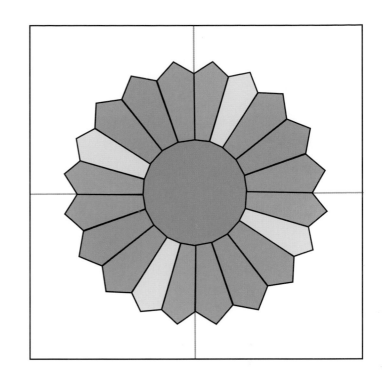

3. Center Circle on Plate.

4. Press in place with steam.

5. Pin each wedge.

6. Sew around Wedges and Circle.

   Machine: *Place invisible thread on top, and loosen top tension. Place thread matching Background in bobbin. Sew around Circle and Wedges with blind hem stitch.*

   Hand: *Sew around Circle and Wedges with hidden applique stitch.*

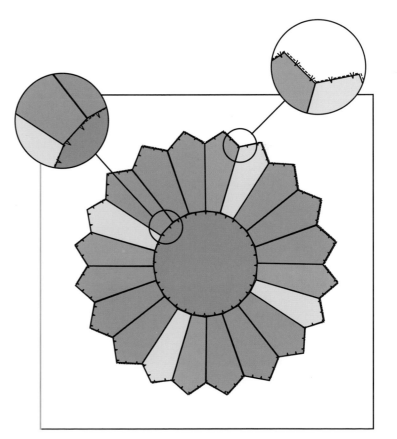

7. Square up block.

Sampler One	**Sampler Two**
12" Block	18" Block
Square to 12½".	Square to 18½".

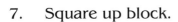

Dresden Plate Quilt Yardage Charts

Finished Block Size 12" square	Wallhanging 2 x 2 = 4 Blocks 43" x 43"	Lap 3 x 4 = 12 Blocks 60" x 75"
Background for Blocks	⅞ yd 　(2) 13" strips cut into 　　(4) 13" squares	1⅝ yds 　(4) 13" strips cut into 　　(12) 13" squares
Five Medium to Dark Wedges Cut from each	¼ yd each 　(1) 4¼" strip each cut into 　　(16) stacks of wedges	½ yd each 　(3) 4¼" strips each cut into 　　(48) stacks of wedges
Circles	¼ yd 　(4) 5½" squares	⅓ yd 　(2) 5½" strips cut into 　　(12) 5½" squares
Non-woven Fusible Interfacing	¼ yd 　(1) 5½" strip cut into 　　(4) 5½" squares	½ yd 　(3) 5½" strips cut into 　　(12) 5½" squares
Inside Lattice Strip	¼ yd 　(4) 1½" strips	⅝ yd 　(11) 1½" strips
Outside Lattice Strips	½ yd 　(8) 1½" strips	1 yd 　(22) 1½" strips
Nine-Patch *Four Squares* 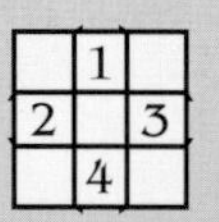	⅛ yd 　(2) 1½" strips 　Cut in half	¼ yd 　(4) 1½" strips 　Cut in half
Nine-Patch *Five Squares* 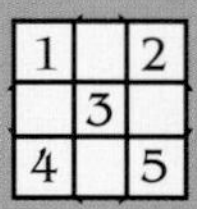	⅛ yd 　(2) 1½" strips 　Cut in half	¼ yd 　(5) 1½" strips 　Cut in half
First Border	⅞ yd 　(5) 5½" strips	1⅓ yds 　(7) 6½" strips
Second Border		
Backing	2⅞ yds	4 yds
Binding	½ yd 　(5) 3" strips	⅔ yd 　(7) 3" strips
Batting	50" x 50"	68" x 83"

Twin	Full/Queen	King
3 x 5 = 15 Blocks **60" x 90"**	**5 x 6 = 30 Blocks** **102" x 117"**	**6 x 6 = 36 Blocks** **117" x 117"**

2 yds
  (5) 13" strips cut into
    (15) 13" squares
	3¾ yds
	  (10) 13" strips cut into
	    (30) 13" squares
		4¾ yds
		  (12) 13" strips cut into
		    (36) 13" squares

½ yd each
  (3) 4¼" strips each cut into
    (60) stacks of wedges
	⅞ yd each
	  (6) 4¼" strips each cut into
	    (120) stacks of wedges
		1 yd each
		  (7) 4¼" strips each cut into
		    (144) stacks of wedges

½ yd each
  (3) 5½" strips each cut into
    (15) 5½" squares
	⅞ yd each
	  (5) 5½" strips each cut into
	    (30) 5½" squares
		1 yd each
		  (6) 5½" strips each cut into
		    (36) 5½" squares

⅔ yd
  (4) 5½" strips cut into
    (15) 5½" squares
	1¼ yds
	  (8) 5½" strips cut into
	    (30) 5½" squares
		1⅓ yds
		  (9) 5½" strips cut into
		    (36) 5½" squares

⅔ yd
  (13) 1½" strips
	1⅛ yds
	  (24) 1½" strips
		1¼ yds
		  (28) 1½" strips

1¼ yds
  (26) 1½" strips
	2⅛ yds
	  (48) 1½" strips
		2½ yds
		  (56) 1½" strips

¼ yd
  (4) 1½" strips
  Cut in half
	½ yd
	  (6) 1½" strips
	  Cut in half
		½ yd
		  (8) 1½" strips
		  Cut in half

¼ yd
  (5) 1½" strips
  Cut in half
	½ yd
	  (8) 1½" strips
	  Cut in half
		½ yd
		  (10) 1½" strips
		  Cut in half

1⅝ yds
  (8) 6½" strips
	1½ yds
	  (9) 5½" strips
		1¾ yds
		  (11) 5½" strips

	2½ yds
	  (11) 7½" strips
		2½ yds
		  (11) 7½" strips

5½ yds	9½ yds	10½ yds

¾ yd
  (8) 3" strips
	1⅛ yds
	  (12) 3" strips
		1⅛ yds
		  (12) 3" strips

68" x 98"	110" x 125"	125" x 125"

Dresden Plate Quilts

Selecting Fabric

Select one Background that reads solid from a distance, and five medium to dark prints for wedges in varying values and scales. Circle fabric can be one of the wedge fabrics or a "fussy cut" design that fits inside a 4½" circle. Calculate yardage by counting out a "fussy cut" for each block.

Select two or three fabrics for Lattice and Cornerstones. In this quilt, three fabrics were selected. The Inside Lattice is Background, Outside Lattice is green, and Nine-Patches combine rose and green, with four squares of green, and five squares of rose.

*Victorian Dresden Plate Quilt
Pieced by Patricia Knoechel
Quilted by Judy Jackson
61" x 69"*

*Laura and
Clint Williams*

Olga Gunn Photography

Scrappy

Select one Background fabric that reads solid from a distance to give unity to the blocks. For a truly scrappy look, select twenty different fabrics for wedges. Sizes Twin and smaller need twenty different ⅛ yd pieces for plates cut into one 4¼" strip each. Queen and King need twenty ¼ yd pieces cut into two 4¼" strips each. Sew wedges together in random order.

In this quilt, the Inside Lattice is green, Outside Lattice is Background, and Nine-Patches combine the same two fabrics, with four squares of Background, and five squares of green.

*Sunflower Quilt
Pieced by Brenda Richmond
Quilted by Sandy Thompson
54" x 68"*

For her daughter's wedding, Brenda created a quilt designed with Laura's favorite flower, the Sunflower. To perfectly frame her artistry, Brenda sewed a folded green border in her binding.

Making Blocks

1. Cut total number of wedges listed in each yardage chart, and sew together.

2. Make total number of blocks as listed.

Making Nine-Patches

In the two quilts on the left, the Lattice and Nine-Patches are opposite in values.

Victorian

Sunflower

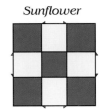

Cut 1½" strips for Nine-Patches in half.

1. Place this many half strips in each stack.

Wallhanging	2
Lap	4
Twin	4
Full/Queen	7
King	8

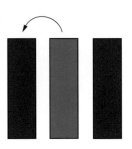
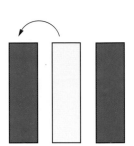

2. Assembly-line sew first two stacks of strips together.

3. Press seams as illustrated.

4. Assembly-line sew third stack.

5. Press as illustrated.

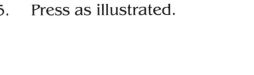

6. Place on cutting mat. Square left end. Cut into this many 1½" sections.

Wallhanging	18
Lap	40
Twin	48
Full/Queen	84
King	98

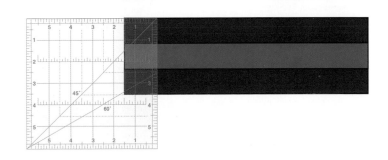

7. Place this many half strips in each stack.

Wallhanging	1
Lap	2
Twin	2
Full/Queen	4
King	4

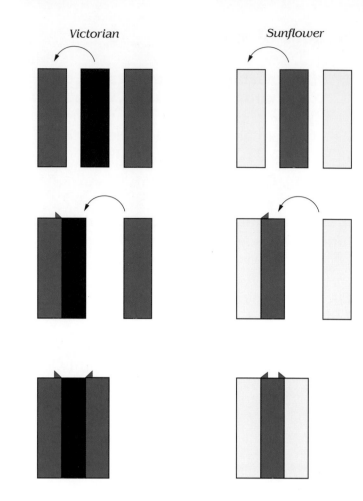

Victorian   Sunflower

8. Assembly-line sew first two stacks of strips together.

9. Press seams as illustrated.

10. Assembly-line sew third stack.

11. Press as illustrated.

12. Place on cutting mat. Square left end. Cut into this many 1½" sections.

Wallhanging	9
Lap	20
Twin	24
Full/Queen	42
King	49

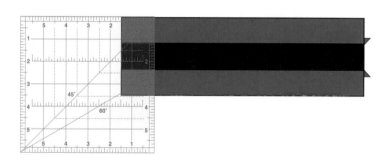

13. Sew this many Nine-Patches together.

Wallhanging	9
Lap	20
Twin	24
Full/Queen	42
King	49

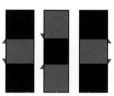

Victorian

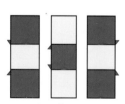

Sunflower

14. Press as illustrated.

Press final seams toward center.

Press final seams away from center.

Sewing Lattice Strips

Victorian   *Sunflower*

Do not cut 1½" Lattice strips in half.

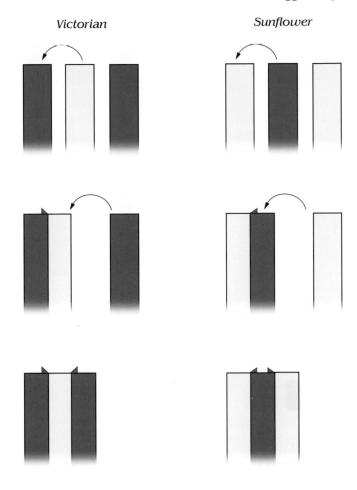

1. Place this many selvage to selvage strips in each stack.

Outside/Inside/Outside	
Wallhanging	4
Lap	11
Twin	13
Full/Queen	24
King	28

2. Assembly-line sew first two stacks of strips together.

3. Press seams as illustrated.

4. Assembly-line sew third stack.

5. Press as ilustrated.

6. Cut into this many 12½" sections.

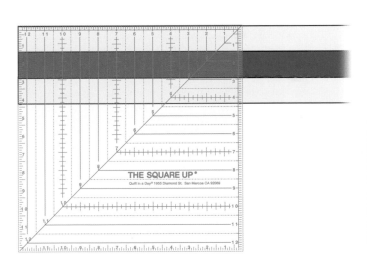

Number of 12¹/₂" Sections	
Wallhanging	12
Lap	31
Twin	38
Full/Queen	71
King	84

7. Lay out with Lattice and Cornerstones between blocks.

Blocks Across and Down	
Wallhanging	2 x 2
Lap	3 x 4
Twin	3 x 5
Full/Queen	5 x 6
King	6 x 6

8. Turn to *Sewing Blocks Together* on page 202.

9. Press seams toward Lattice.

Holiday Wreath

Pieced by Eleanor Burns
Quilted by Amie Potter
26" x 26"

Background ⅔ yd
(1) 19" square

Five Medium to Dark Green ¼ yd each
(1) 6" x 12" from each

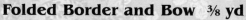

Folded Border and Bow ⅜ yd
(4) 1¼" x 19" for Folded Border
(1) 9" x 34" for Bow
(1) 4" x 6½" for Bow

Border and Binding ¾ yd
(2) 4¼" x 19"
(2) 4¼" x 26½"
(3) 3" strips

Backing ⅞ yd
(1) 30" square

Batting 30" square

Supplies

❏ Stiletto

❏ 6" x 12" Ruler

❏ Applique Foot

❏ Permanent
Marking Pen

❏ Invisible Thread

Making Holiday Wreath

1. Follow directions on pages 86-88 for making 18" Sampler Two block using five different greens.

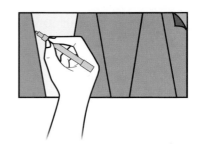

2. Staystitch around inside circle with ¼" seam from raw edge with green thread.

3. Turn under on ¼" seam.

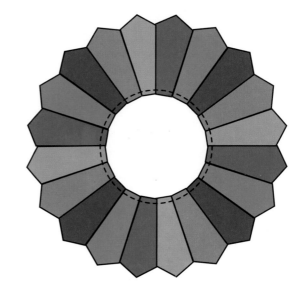

4. Press Background square in half, and half again into quarters.

5. Carefully center Wreath on Background square, lining up seams with folds.

    For a balanced look, place dominant colored wedge in some position as darkest green.

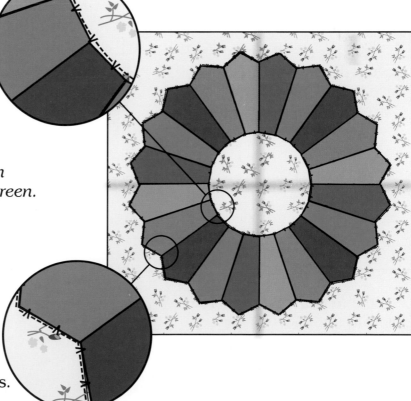

6. **Machine:** Place invisible thread on top, and loosen top tension. Place thread matching Background in bobbin. Sew inside Circle and around Wedges with blind hem stitch.

    Hand: Use applique stitches.

Making Folded Border

1. Press 1¼" strips in half lengthwise, wrong sides together.

2. Place Folded Border on two opposite sides, matching raw edges. Sew ⅛" from raw edges with 10 stitches per inch or #3 setting. Trim even with sides of top. **Do not fold out**.

3. Repeat on remaining two sides.

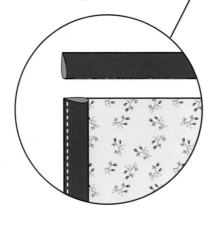

Making Bow

1. Fold 9" x 34" strip right sides together. On fold, mark 1½" in on both ends. Draw lines from 1½" marks to ¼" in on opposite sides. Mark 3" opening in center.

2. Sew on diagonal lines and long side, leaving 3" open.

3. Trim ends. Turn right side out. Pick out points.

4. Fold in half, and draw a line 9" from fold. Sew on line.

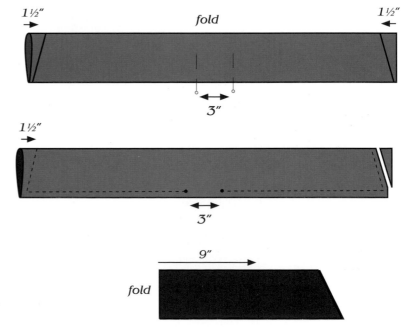

5. Bring center fold to match just sewn seam.

6. Fold 4" x 6½" strip in half right sides together. Sew long side. Turn right side out. Press with seam centered.

7. Wrap center strip around Bow, and sew ends together.

8. Sew to Wreath.

9. Turn to **Adding Borders**, page 220.

Buttermilk Hotcakes

3 cupfuls all-purpose flour
3 tablespoonfuls white sugar
3 teaspoonfuls baking powder
1 1/2 teaspoonfuls baking soda
3/4 teaspoonful salt

3 cupfuls buttermilk
1/2 cupful milk
3 eggs
1/3 cupful butter, melted

In a large bowl, combine flour, sugar, baking powder, baking soda, and salt. In a separate bowl, beat together buttermilk, milk, eggs and melted butter. Keep the two mixtures separate until you are ready to cook.

Heat a lightly oiled griddle or frying pan over medium high heat. You can flick water across the surface and if it beads up and sizzles, it's ready!

Pour the wet mixture into the dry mixture, using a wooden spoon or fork to blend. Stir until it's just blended together. Do not over stir! Pour or scoop the batter onto the griddle, using approximately 1/2 cup for each hotcake. Brown on both sides and serve hot with butter and syrup. Makes about 12 hotcakes.

Christmas Memories

Christmas in the 1930's was a time when there was very little money and few jobs. Folks were never so poor that there wasn't at least one gift for everyone as a sled, ice skates, cowboy boots, or book. The Christmas tree was put up on Christmas Eve. When everyone got up in the morning, the tree would be decorated with candles and cookies baked the day before. Many received an orange they got only at Christmas. That orange, with hotcakes made from scratch, made Christmas complete!

Antique quilt from collection
of Eleanor Burns

In the 1930's many
marriages were postponed
because, with the
Depression, couples did
not have the necessary
funds to get married and
set up housekeeping.
If wedding plans
proceeded, a groom
could pick up a blue-
white diamond for only
$25, with a free 18
carat gold wedding
band thrown in. The
bride often wore a
slim fitting suit or
drop shoulder satin
dress with full length
gloves and a hat
with a netted face
veil, seamed nylons,
and spiked heeled
shoes. The groom
attired himself in a
pin striped suit!

Double Wedding Ring

Also known as

- *Endless Chain*
- *Rainbow*
- *Around the World*
- *King Tut*
- *Double Wedding Bands*

Sampler One
One 12" Block
Finished Size

Background
(1) 13" square

Six Medium to Dark
(1) 3" x 10" strip from each

Corners
(2) 4" squares

Double Wedding Ring from Quiltsmart®
(1 panel)
or **Fusible Interfacing**
(1) 12" square

Sampler Two
Three 12" Blocks
Finished Size

Background
(3) 13" squares

Six Medium to Dark
(1) 3" x 30" strip from each
or
(3) 3" x 10" strips from each

Corners
(6) 4" squares

Double Wedding Ring from Quiltsmart®
(1 panel)
or **Fusible Interfacing**
(1) 18" x 20"

Supplies

❑ Permanent Marking Pen

❑ 6" Hemostat or Longer

❑ Hera Marker or Chalk

❑ Invisible Thread

❑ Wooden Iron or Non-Stick Applique Pressing Sheet

❑ Double Wedding Ring Pieced Arc Template from Quiltsmart® *(Optional)*

Double Wedding Ring

5) Assemble by ironing in place on 12" square of background fabric. (Center using marks: ^)
6) Sew arcs to block - narrow zigzag is recommended.
7) Add corner triangles: Place 2-½" square in each corner, stitch across diagonal.

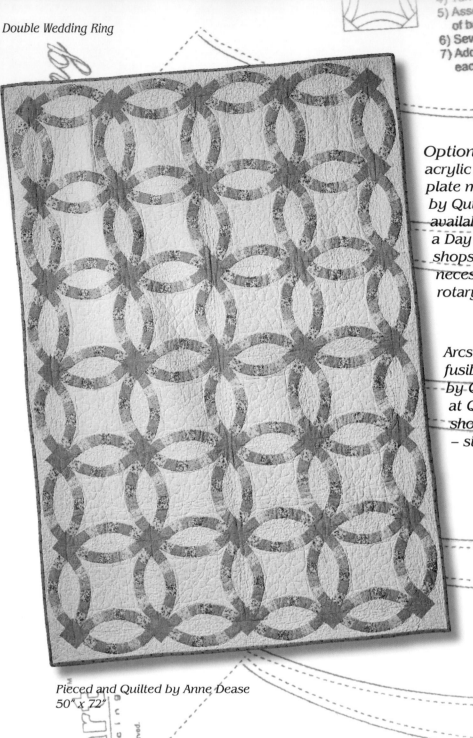

Pieced and Quilted by Anne Dease
50" x 72"

Optional: A heavy acrylic wedge template manufactured by Quiltsmart™ is available at Quilt in a Day and other quilt shops. No marking is necessary – simply rotary cut wedges.

Arcs printed on non-woven fusible interfacing manufactured by Quiltsmart® are also available at Quilt in a Day and other quilt shops. No tracing is necessary – simply cut arcs apart.

See *Double Wedding Ring* from Quiltsmart® for complete yardage and sewing instructions for this quilt.
If your local quilt shop does not carry these products, contact Quiltsmart®.

www.quiltsmart.com
email@quiltsmart.com

952.445.5737
888.446.5750 (Toll Free US & Canada)
Fax to 952.445.2136

Cutting Wedges

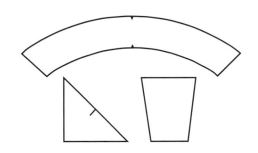

1. Find wedge, arc, and corner Double Wedding Ring templates found in back of book, and remove.

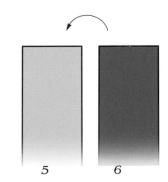

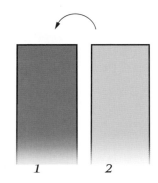

2. Lay out six different 3" strips in preferred color order.

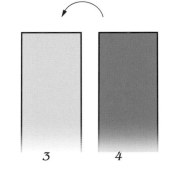

3. Starting on left side, flip 2 right sides together to 1. Flip 4 to 3. Flip 6 to 5.

4. Working from left to right, stack strips. Keep 1/2 on top, and 5/6 on bottom. Pieces are now stacked in their cutting and sewing order.

5. Trace wedges with permanent marking pen.

   Sampler One   **Sampler Two**
   (4) wedges   (12) wedges

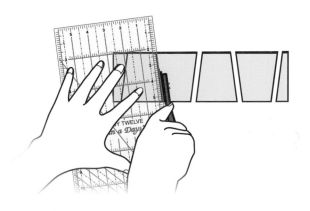

6. Layer cut with 6" x 12" ruler.
   Optional: Cut wedges with Quiltsmart® template.

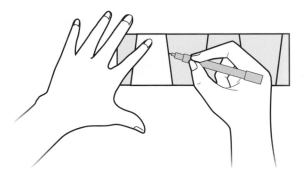

Sewing Wedges

1. Pick up pairs as they are stacked.

2. Assembly-line sew 1 and
    2 into pairs, 3 and 4 into
    pairs, and 5 and 6 into pairs.
    Clip apart and open.

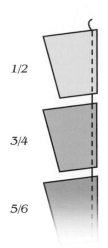

3. Assembly-line sew 1/2
    and 3/4 together.

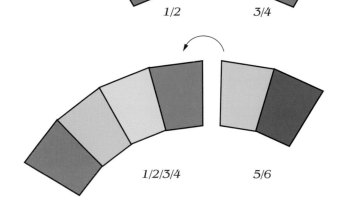

4. Assembly-line sew 1/2/3/4
    and 5/6 together. Clip apart.

5. From wrong side, press seams to left.

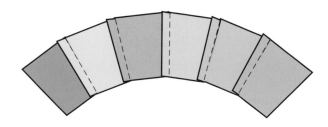

Tracing and Sewing Arcs

1. Trace arc template on smooth side of non-woven fusible interfacing with permanent marking pen. Mark center notches. Leave ½" space between pieces.

    Sampler One   **Sampler Two**
    (4) arcs   (12) arcs

    Optional: Use 1 panel Quiltsmart® printed interfacing.

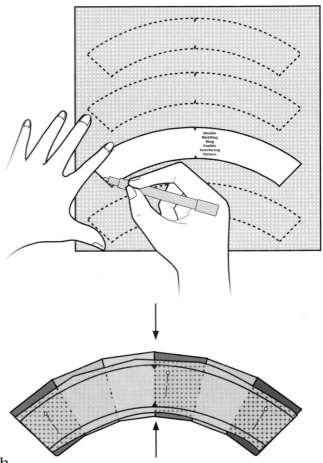

2. Rough cut around arcs on fusible interfacing.

3. Place interfacing arc on wedges, with rough fusible side against right side of wedges. Match notch on interfacing with center seam on wedges. Pin in place.

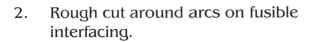

Match notch with center of arc.

4. Place open toe applique foot on sewing machine. Lighten pressure on presser foot.

5. Sew on curved solid line with 18 stitches per inch, or 1.8 on computerized machine. If available, use needle down position on needle.

6. Leave ends open for turning.

7. Sew on remaining curved side in same direction so underneath seams do not flip.

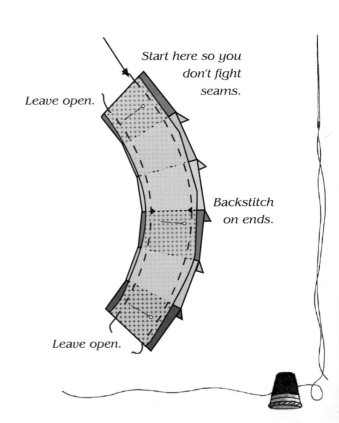

Start here so you don't fight seams.

Leave open.

Backstitch on ends.

Leave open.

Trimming and Turning Arcs

1.   Trim ⅛" away from stitching.
     Trim ends.

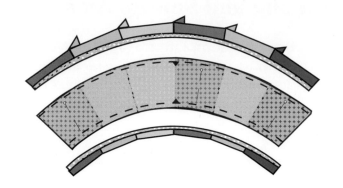

2.   Insert hemostat in open end, push
     tip of hemostat to opposite end, and
     firmly grasp fabric. Carefully turn arc
     right side out.

3.   Run hemostat around inside
     edge of each piece.

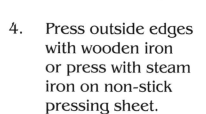

4.   Press outside edges
     with wooden iron
     or press with steam
     iron on non-stick
     pressing sheet.

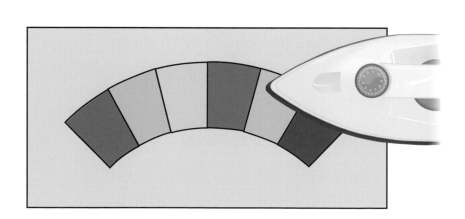

Sewing Arcs

1. Press 13" Background square in half, and half again into quarters.

2. Line up corner template in corners and draw diagonal lines. Mark centers.

   There are two corner templates. Make sure you use the larger of the two templates.

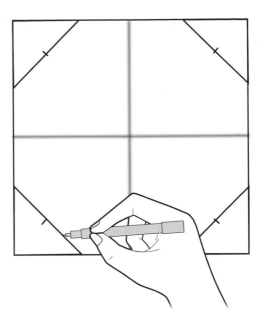

3. Line up center seams on arcs with folds on Background square. In corners, line up edges of arcs with center marks. *Some arcs may be longer and extend past diagonal line.*

4. Fuse in place with steam, first from right side, and then from wrong side.

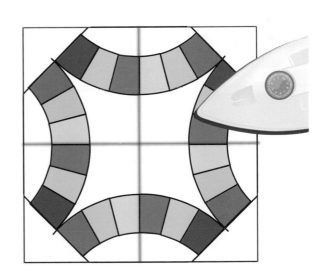

5. Sew continuously around inside edges of arcs. Sew outside edges. If interfacing shows, guide it under arc with stiletto and stitch over.

   Machine: *Use blind hem stitch that bites to left, #9 needle, and invisible thread. Loosen top tension. Use bobbin thread to match Background.*

   Hand: *Use applique stitches.*

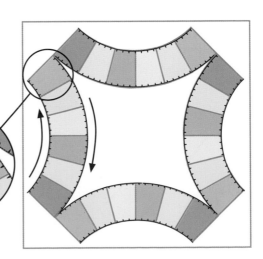

Adding Corners

1. Cut 4" Corner squares in half on one diagonal.

2. Press triangles in half.

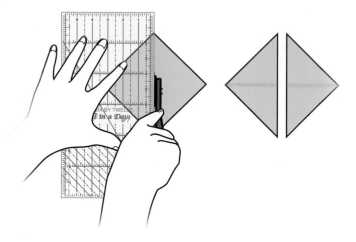

3. Place triangles right sides together with arcs. Line up with lines on Background. Sew ¼" seam.

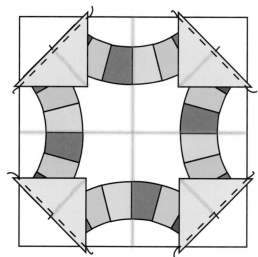

The arcs may cover some of the line. Use the ends of the line for triangle placement.

4. Open triangles, and press.

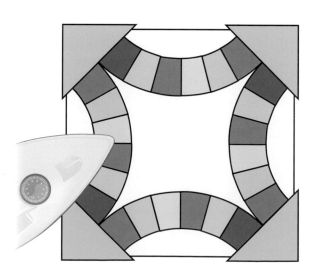

5. Lightly draw one diagonal line across block with chalk, hera marker, or disappearing pen.

6. Center 12½" Square Up Ruler on block. Line up ruler's diagonal line through centers of two sets of arcs. Check to see that corners of ruler line up with marked diagonal line.

7. Square block to 12½".

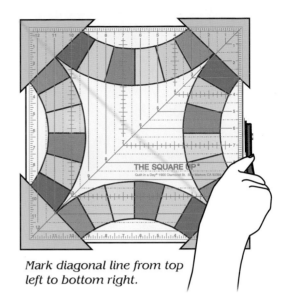

Mark diagonal line from top left to bottom right.

Optional: Sew two different colors on Corners opposite each other.

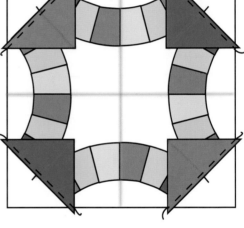

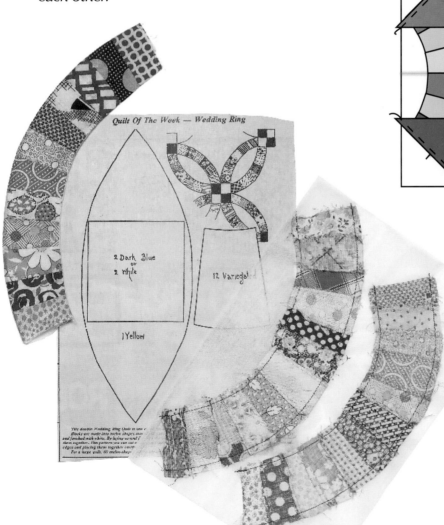

Finishing Antique Arcs

Pieces of Double Wedding Ring quilts can often be found in antique stores and flea markets. Arcs can be finished with this same method. Pin right side of arc to fusible side of interfacing, sew long sides, trim, and turn. Experiment with four arcs on one Background square to determine what size Background square and Corner square to cut.

Double Wedding Ring Tablerunner

*Holiday Tablerunner Pieced
and Quilted by Brenda Witt
20" x 43"*

Background 1 yd
(1) 12½" strip cut into
    (3) 12½" squares
(3) 5" strips cut into
    (8) 5" x 12½" rectangles
    (4) 5" squares

Six Different Fat Quarters
(2) 3" half strips from each

Corners from Favorite Fat Quarter
(3) 3½" half strips cut into
    (16) 3½" squares

Non-woven Fusible Interfacing 1¼ yds
or
Double Wedding Ring panels
from Quiltsmart® (2 panels)

One Fabric Binding ⅜ yd
(4) 3" strips
or
Scrappy Binding
    (6) 3" half strips cut from fat quarters

Backing 1⅓ yds

Batting 27" x 50"

Supplies
❑ Stiletto
❑ Wooden Iron
❑ 12½" Square Up Ruler

*1930's Reproduction Tablerunner Pieced by Eleanor Burns
Quilted by Teresa Varnes
20" x 43"*

*Fabric is Aunt Grace's Scrapbag from the collection
of Judie Rothermel for Marcus Brothers Textiles, Inc.®*

Cutting Twenty Stacks of Wedges

1. Layer 3" half strips in pairs right sides together following directions beginning on page 103.

2. Cut 20 stacks of wedges.

   Depending on the lengths of the 3" half strips, you may get only 18 stacks. If necessary, layer additional fabric and cut the last wedges.

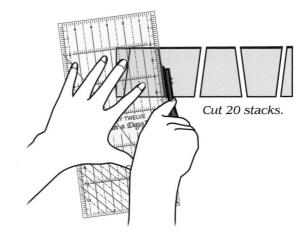

Cut 20 stacks.

Sewing Twenty Arcs

1. Sew twenty arcs together.

   Background squares for Tablerunner are 12½" square and Corner squares are 3½" square, as opposed to 13" Background squares and 4" Corner squares for Sampler quilts.

2. Make three blocks, substituting Tablerunner measurements.

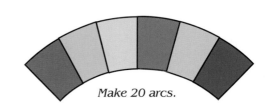

Make 20 arcs.

Square Three Blocks to 12" Square

1. Center 12½" Square Up Ruler on block. Line up ruler's diagonal line through centers of two sets of arcs.

2. Place ¼" lines on ends of arcs. Trim right and top edges.

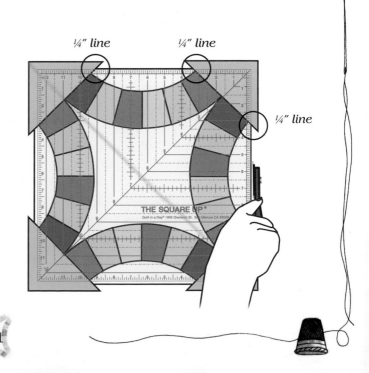

¼" line   ¼" line

¼" line

THE SQUARE UP®
Quilt in a Day® 1955 Diamond St. San Marcos CA 92069

3. Turn block. Do not turn ruler. Place ruler's 12" line on left and bottom edges of block. Make sure ¼" lines touch seams on right and top edges. Trim right and top edges.

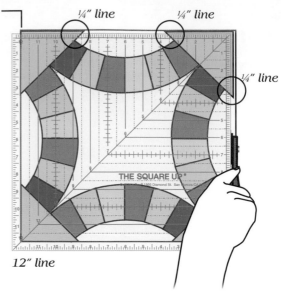

12" line

12" line

4. Lift Corner triangles, and trim Background ¼" from seam.

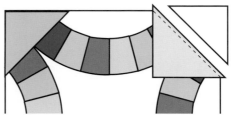

Making Eight Side Rectangles

1. Find Tablerunner template in back of book, and remove.

2. Mark two corners on each 5" x 12½" Background rectangle with template.

3. Fold rectangle in half and press.

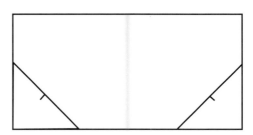

4. Line up one arc with center seam on fold, and marks on corners. Steam press in place from right and wrong side.

   Some arcs may be longer and extend past diagonal lines.

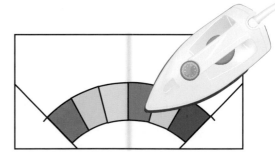

5. Sew edges of arc in place with invisible thread and blind hem stitch.

6. Cut 3½" Corner squares in half on one diagonal. Fingerpress triangles in half.

7. Place two triangle Corners right sides together with arc. Line up with lines on Background. Sew ¼" seam.

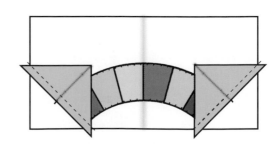

8. Open triangles, and press.

9. Square rectangles to 4¾" x 12". *Place 12½" ruler's diagonal line against right seam, and ¼" line against two top seams.*

10. Trim right and top edges.

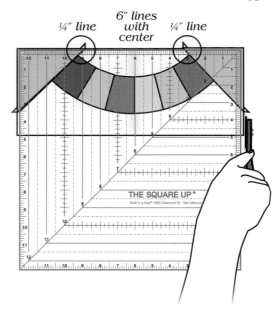

11. Turn rectangle. Do not turn ruler. Place 12" line on left edge, and 4¾" line on bottom edge. Trim right and top edges.

12. Lift Corner triangles, and trim Background ¼" from seam.

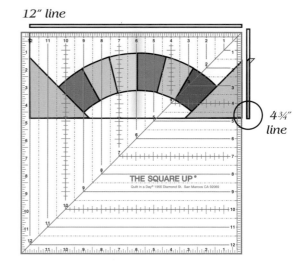

Making Four Triangle Corners

For plain corners like the Holiday Tablerunner, square the 5" Background squares to 4¾". Skip these steps.

1. Draw one diagonal line with Tablerunner template in corner of 5" Background squares.

2. Fingerpress Corner triangle in half. Line up Corner triangle right sides together to line on 5" Background square, and assembly-line sew.

3. Open Corner triangle and press.

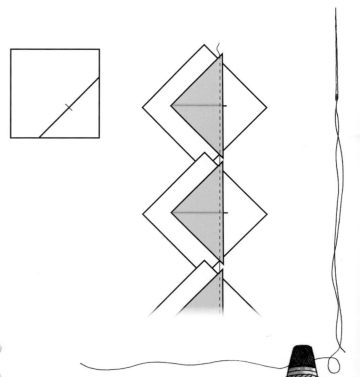

4. Trim patch to 4⅞". *Place 6" Square Up Ruler's 4⅞" line on left and bottom edges. Trim right and top edges.*

5. Turn patch. Do not turn ruler. Square to 4¾".

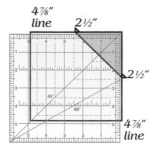
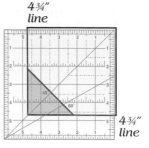

Trim patch to 4⅞".　　　Square patch to 4¾".

Sewing Tablerunner Together

1. Lay out pieces.

2. Flip middle vertical row right sides together to left vertical row. Match and pin seams at Corner triangles.

3. Sew vertical row together.

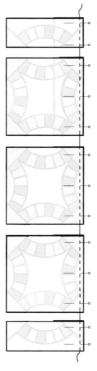

4. Flip right vertical row right sides together to middle vertical row. Match and pin seams at Corners.

5. Sew vertical row together.

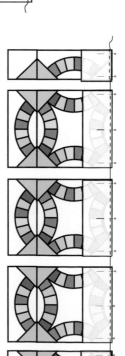

6. Clip rows apart. Press rows as illustrated.

7. If necessary, sliver trim triangles to straighten.

8. Pin and sew remaining rows.

9. Press just sewn seams toward center.

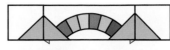
seams in

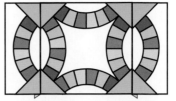
seams out

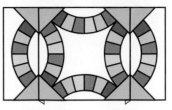
seams in

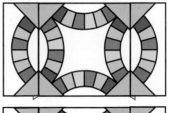
seams out

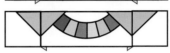
seams in

Scrappy Binding

1. Turn to page 224 for *Layering Your Quilt*.

2. Trace 8" stencil in center area and free motion quilt, following directions on page 227.

3. Stitch in the ditch around arcs, and ¼" away.

4. Piece 3" half strips into one long strip for Scrappy Binding.

5. Turn to page 228 for *Binding*.

The 8" stencil used for free motion quilting is from the Stencil Company, SCL-132-08.

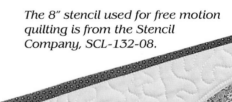

*Antique Quilt from collection
of Eleanor Burns*

Southwest Kansas
and Panhandle
Oklahoma were the
most drastically
affected areas during
the Dust Bowl of the
1930's. There were
impenetrable clouds
of red, yellow, and
brown gritty dust
swirling across
the countryside,
carrying with it
topsoil, seed,
and the hope of
the Great Plains
farmers. The heat
was inescapable
in mid-summer.
On black days
when the dust was
heavy enough that
the family had to
light the lamps
at noon, the
chickens would
go to roost, and
wouldn't lay
eggs.

Rocky Road
to Kansas
Also known as

- Kite
- String

116

Samplers One and Two
One 12" Block Finished Size
for each Sampler

Background
(1) 3¾" strip

String Triangles
Narrow scraps or
Six Medium to Dark
(1) 7" square from each
cut into
(1) 2" x 7" strip
(2) 1¼" x 7" strips
(1) 1½" x 7" strip
(1) 1" x 7" strip

Medium Corners
(1) 4" square

Dark Corners
(1) 4" square

Muslin ¼ yard
(1) 7" x 14" strip

Supplies

❑ Fine Point Permanent
Marking Pen

❑ Stiletto

❑ Pins

❑ 6" x 12" Ruler

❑ 6½" Triangle
Square Up Ruler

Tracing Templates

1. Find String Triangle and Background Triangle templates in back of book, and remove.

2. On Background Triangle, push thumb tack or stiletto through dot and make a small hole.

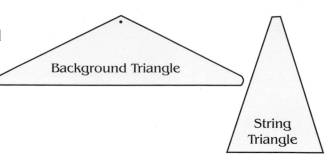

Cutting Pieces from Background Triangle Template

1. Turn 3¾" Background strip wrong side up.

2. Line up template with strip. Trace four Background Triangles on 3¾" strip with fine point permanent pen.

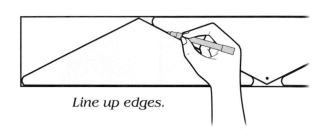

Line up edges.

3. Mark dot through hole on wrong side of each Background Triangle.

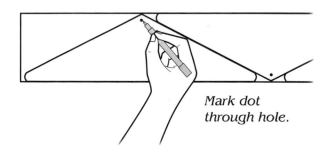

Mark dot through hole.

4. Cut straight lines with ruler and cutter. Cut curved lines with scissors.

5. Check Background Triangles against template.

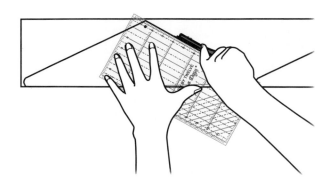

Cutting String Triangles

1. Trace four String Triangles on 7" x 14" muslin strip with triangle template.

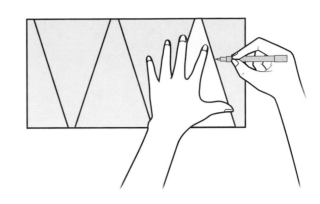

2. Cut String Triangles with ruler and cutter.

3. Check muslin triangles against template, especially tops of triangles.

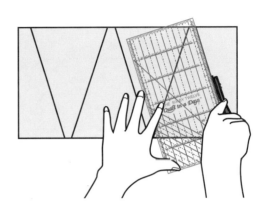

Making String Triangles

1. Place 1½" wide strip across bottom of muslin triangle right side up.

2. Place second strip of any width and different fabric **on angle** right sides together to first strip.

3. Sew ¼" seam.

4. Sew strips to all four muslin triangles in different fabrics. Sew one at a time, or assembly-line sew.

5. Open and fingerpress.

6. Rough cut strips from muslin side. Use trimmed strips for covering tops of Triangles.

7. Place third strip right sides together to second strip **on angle**, and sew.

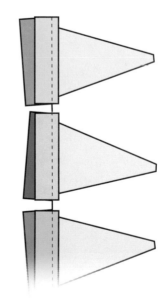

Trim pieces slightly longer than triangle as you sew. Use trimmed strips where they fit.

119

8. Continue until muslin triangle is covered with strips. **Finish with wide strip at top.**

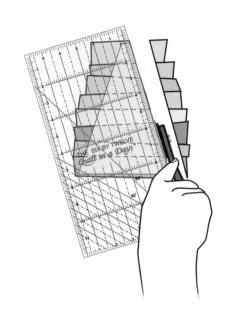

9. Place string triangle template on wrong side of muslin triangles. Since muslin tends to stretch, draw new lines if necessary.

10. Trim strips from wrong side of muslin triangles.

11. Check against template.

Adding 4" Corner Squares

1. Cut 4" medium and dark squares in half on one diagonal.

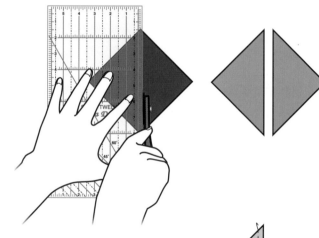

2. Lay out String Triangles and plan placement with Corner triangles.

3. Center Corners right sides together on String Triangles, and assembly-line sew ¼" seam.

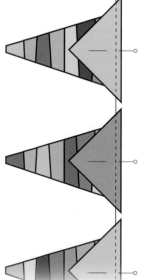

4. Press seams on dark Corners toward dark.

5. Press medium Corners toward String Triangles.

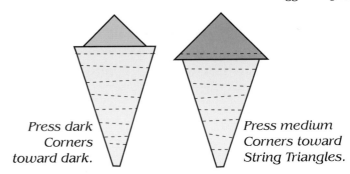

Press dark Corners toward dark.

Press medium Corners toward String Triangles.

6. From right side, place 3½" line on 6½" Triangle Square Up Ruler **on seam**. Trim on two sides.

7. Trim tips on medium Corners.

*From right side, place 3½" line on 6½" Triangle Square Up Ruler **on seam**.*

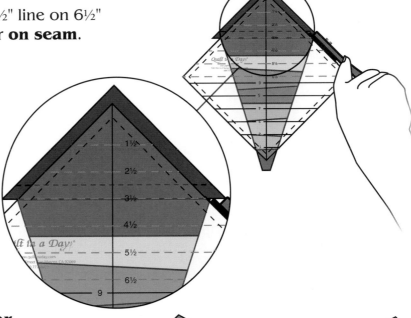

Sewing Pieces Together

1. Lay out four pieces. Place medium and dark Corners opposite each other.

2. Flip pieces on right onto pieces on left, right sides together.

3. Assembly-line sew.

4. Turn, and sew remaining row. At connecting thread, push top seam up, and underneath seam down.

5. Clip connecting thread, and lay block flat wrong side up.

6. Press center open into four-patch.

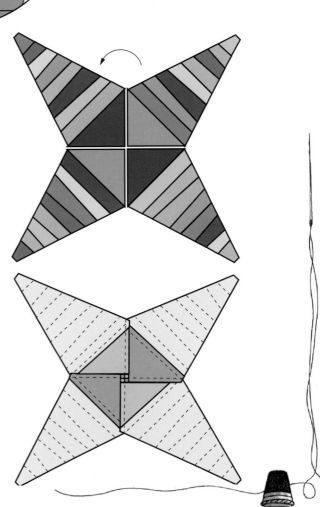

Adding Background Triangles

1. Place four Background Triangles with String Triangles.

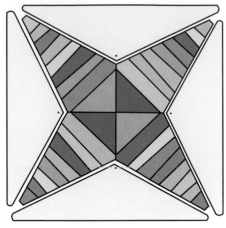

2. Flip Background right sides together to String Triangle. Match rounded ends. Pin through Background dot to seam on Corner Triangles. Sew from rounded end and stop at dot.

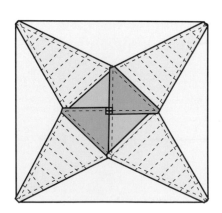

Pivot on dot

3. Using needle down position, pivot to next side and line up edges. Pin. Use stiletto to help match edges to end.

4. Sew from dot to end of String Triangle.

5. Press seam toward Background.

6. Sew next three Background Triangles.

7. Square to 12½".

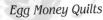

Jeanne Crone sent this unfinished piece to Eleanor Burns, along with the photographs and letter. The patchwork was pieced by Etta Robinson Bowen Kiggins, 1877-1965, the grandmother, and Pearl Bowen Nunn, 1900-1986, the daughter.

No wonder the ladies didn't finish their quilt! It was just too hard to put together! The pieces are Rocky Road to Kansas, set together without Background Triangles. Someday, Eleanor plans to sew the String Triangles together with black Background Triangles. Someday!

"The farm home in Michigan is sad. Later, pictured with a porch that was put on when renovated. The porch was added so that when she died, (Etta) she did not want to be taken out of the house through the kitchen."

Yes, I warned you that this was an unsightly partial quilt. My friend, whose mother and grandmother made this, has moved. For many years she kept it. No one wanted to finish it and she didn't want to throw it away.

Old farmhouse circa 1915 without porch

Etta and Pearl in front of new porch

Etta's Apron

Grandmother Kiggins wore two aprons. The outer apron, a coverall, was flowered, often made of feed bags. If anyone came by to visit, the outer apron was removed before she appeared at the door. The inner apron was white, sparkling clean with it and a great smile, she greated the vistor.

Grandmother Kiggins and Daughter Pearl

31½" x 41"

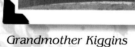

Grandmother Kiggins

Print Fabric 1½ yds
Center Apron
(1) 16" x 42" strip
Sides
(1) 16" strip cut into
(2) 16" x 21"
Ties
(2) 3½" strips
Pockets
(2) 8" x 9½"

Rickrack 5 yds

Supplies

❏ Thread to Match Rickrack

❏ Double Needle for Edgestitching (Optional)

Cutting Out Apron

1. Find two apron pattern pieces in back of book, and cut out.

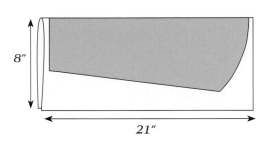

2. Fold two 16" Side pieces in half lengthwise, wrong sides together. Stack.

3. Place Side apron pattern on fold, pin, and cut out.

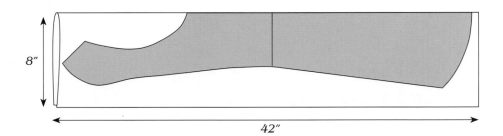

4. Tape Center apron pattern together. Fold 16" Center Apron fabric in half lengthwise, wrong side together.

5. Place Center apron pattern on fold, pin, and cut out.

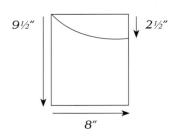

6. Place Pocket pieces right sides together. Mark down 2½" on right side, and draw curved line. Cut on curved line.

Sewing Rickrack

1. Set up machine with thread matching rickrack on top and in bobbin.

2. Place clear open toe foot on sewing machine. Lengthen stitch, and lighten foot pressure.

3. Sew rickrack around outside edge of Center Apron. *You need 2⅔ yards of continuous rickrack for Center Apron.*

4. Sew rickrack to neck of Center Apron.

5. Sew neck seam on Center Apron.

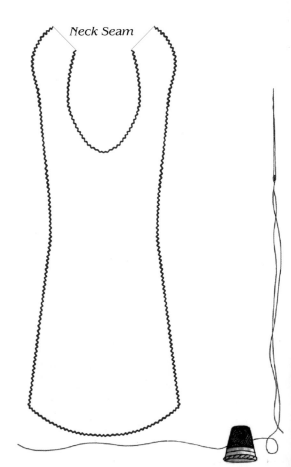

Neck Seam

6. Sew rickrack to curved top edges of Pockets, and curved bottom edges of Sides. Turn rickrack under, press, and edgestitch.

7. Press under two sides on each Pocket and two outside edges of Sides.

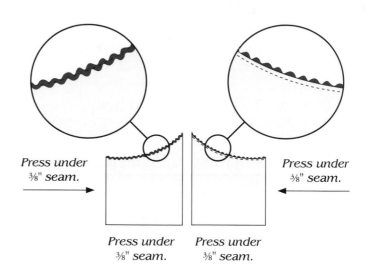

Press under ⅜" seam.   *Press under ⅜" seam.*

Press under ⅜" seam.   *Press under ⅜" seam.*

Sewing Pockets and Sides

1. Pin Pockets in place on Sides 2" down from top edge. Match raw edges.

2. Baste raw edges together with 3.0 stitch length, and edgestitch remaining two turned under sides. Backstitch edges of Pockets.

3. Edgestitch two outside edges of Sides.

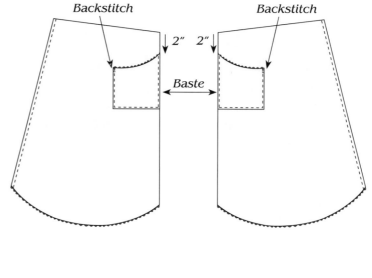

Backstitch   *Backstitch*

2"   2"

Baste

4. Press under two long sides and one narrow end of 3½" Ties.

5. Mark in 11" from narrow end on each Tie. Edgestitch all but 11" section.

6. Fold 3½" strip in half, wrong sides together. Insert Side piece ⅜" into folded section. Pin, catching both edges of 11" section.

7. Sew, backstitching on ends. Ties are left open for a full bow.

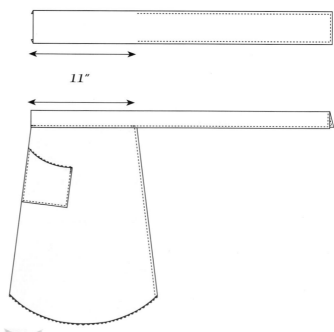

11"

11"

Finishing Apron

1. Lay out Center Apron, right side up. Position Sides.

2. Slide Sides under Center Apron ⅜". Line up bottom scallops. Pin.

3. Edgestitch rickrick around Center Apron, catching Sides at same time.

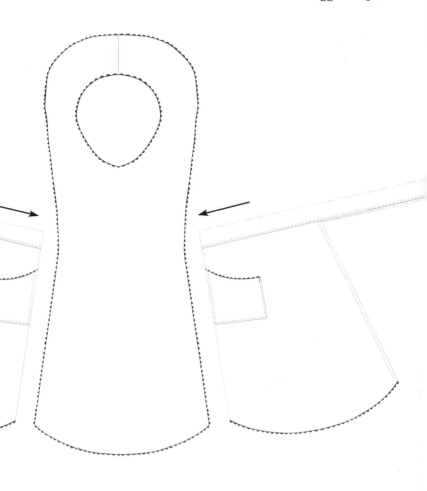

Grandma's Apron

From the chicken coop the apron was used for carrying eggs, fussy chicks, and sometimes half-hatched eggs to be finished in the warming oven.

From the garden it carried all sorts of vegetables. After the peas had been shelled it carried out the hulls.

In the fall it was used to bring in apples that had fallen from the trees.

When unexpected company drove up the road, it was surprising how much furniture that old apron could dust in a matter of seconds.

When dinner was ready, Grandma walked out on the porch and waved her apron, and the men knew it was time to come in from the fields for dinner.

It will be a long time before anyone invents something that will replace that old-time apron that served so many purposes.

127

Antique quilt from collection
of Eleanor Burns

Peonies made quite
a display and were
often at the height of
their bloom during
Commencement in
June. Depression
era women found
peonies to be
beautiful, easy
to grow, and
long lived. The
neighborly thing to
do was take along
a colorful bouquet
to brighten a
friend's day.

In the fall, folks
cut the stems
down, and
dressed them
with well-
rotted chicken
manure!

Peony
Also known as

• *Piney*

• *Double Peony*

• *Yellow Lily Bed of Peonies*

• *Double Tulip Bouquet*

*There are yardage charts and instructions
for two sizes of blocks, two bonus projects
and one Wallhanging. Turn to page 142 for
Wallhanging yardage.*

Sampler One
One 12" Block
Finished Size

Background
(4) 4½" squares
(16) 2" squares
(1) 6½" square

Red Petals
(3) 6" squares
(1) 2" x 9" strip
(1) 2" x 15" strip

Green Petals
(1) 6" square
(1) 2" x 9" strip

Green Leaves
(1) 3½" x 5"

Green Curved Stem
(1) 1" x 11" bias strip
See page 137

Green Center Stem
(1) 1¼" x 12" bias strip

Non-woven Fusible Interfacing
(1) 3½" x 5"

Sampler Two
One 24" Block
Finished Size

Background
(4) 7½" squares
(16) 3½" squares
(1) 12½" square

Red Petals
(3) 9" squares
(3) 3½" x 15" strips

Green Petals
(1) 9" square
(1) 3½" x 15" strip

Green Leaves
(1) 5" x 7½"

Green Curved Stem
(1) 1⅛" x 20" bias strip
See page 137

Green Center Stem
(1) 1¼" x 24" bias strip

Non-woven Fusible Interfacing
(1) 5" x 7½"

Supplies

❏ Permanent Marking Pen

❏ Disappearing Pen

❏ 6" x 24" Ruler

❏ 3" x 6" Flying Geese Ruler

❏ Scrap of Cotton Batting

❏ Thread to match Stem and Leaf Fabric

❏ Hand Sewing Needle

❏ Seam Ripper

❏ Applique Tools:

　❏ Ball Point Bodkin

　❏ Wooden Iron

　❏ Stiletto

　❏ Fat Straw

　❏ Hemostat

Yardage is enough for one complete block, plus one bonus flower.
Turn the bonus flower into a charming pillow or wallhanging. See page 147.

Making Peony Flower
Petals (Flying Geese)

1. Place smaller squares right sides together and centered on larger squares.

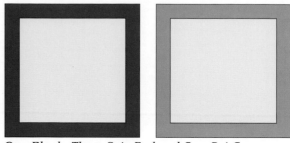

Sampler One
12" Block
(4) 4½" squares
Background

(3) 6" squares red
(1) 6" square green

Sampler Two
24" Block
(4) 7½" squares
Background

(3) 9" squares red
(1) 9" square green

One Block -Three Sets Red and One Set Green
Four Blocks - Nine Sets Red and Three Sets Green

Four Block Wallhanging
(12) 4½" squares Background
(9) 6" squares red
(3) 6" squares green

2. Place 6" x 24" ruler on squares so ruler touches four corners. Draw diagonal line across squares. Pin.

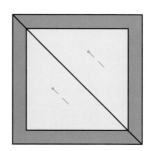

3. Sew exactly ¼" from drawn line. Use 15 stitches per inch or 2.0 on computerized machine. Remove pins. Press to set seam.

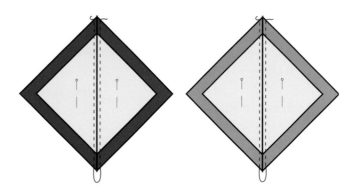

4. Cut on drawn line.

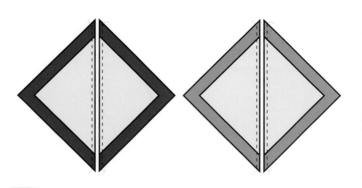

5. Place on pressing mat with large triangle on top. Press to set seam.

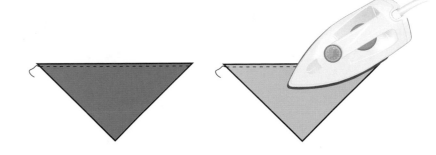

6. Open and press toward larger triangle. Check that there are no folds at seams.

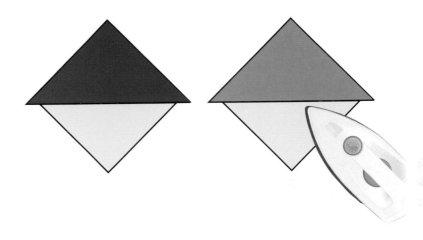

7. Place sets of red pieces right sides together so that opposite fabrics touch. Place sets of red and green right sides together. Seams are parallel with each other.

8. Match up outside edges. Notice the gap between seams. **The seams do not lock.**

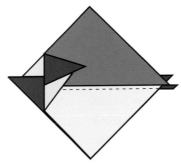
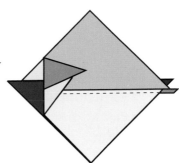

One Block
Make two sets all red.

Four Block Wallhanging
Make six sets all red.

One Block
Make two sets green and red.

Four Block Wallhanging
Make six sets green and red.

9. Draw a diagonal line across seams. Pin. Sew ¼" from both sides of drawn line. Hold seams flat with stiletto so seams do not flip. Press to set seam.

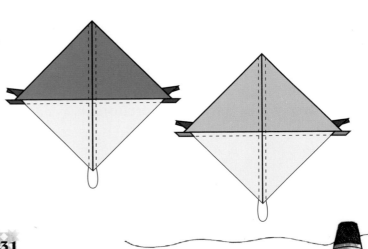

10. Cut on drawn line.

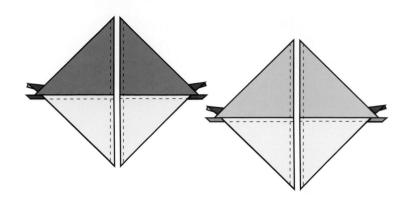

11. Fold in half and clip to the stitching. This allows the seam allowance to be pressed away from the Background triangle.

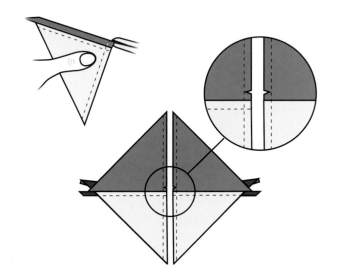

12. From right side, press into one Background triangle. Turn and press into second Background triangle.

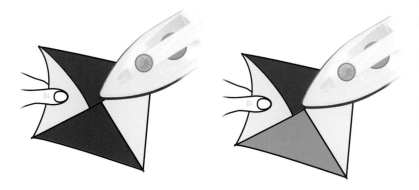

13. Turn over, and press on wrong side. At clipped seam, fabric is pressed in opposite directions.

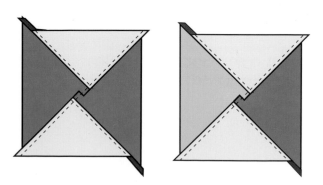

Squaring Up with 3" x 6" Flying Geese Ruler

Put InvisiGrip® on underside of ruler.

Sampler One and Wallhanging

1. Line up ruler's red lines on 45° sewn lines. Line up red dotted line with peak of triangle for ¼" seam allowance. Cut block in half to separate into two patches.

   ### Sampler One
   Square to 2" x 3½"
   Finished Geese is 1½" x 3"

   ### Four Block Wallhanging
   Square to 2" x 3½"
   Finished Geese is 1½" x 3"

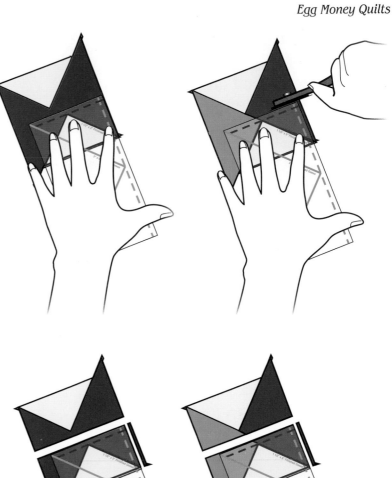

2. Hold ruler securely on fabric so it does not shift while cutting. Trim off excess fabric on right.

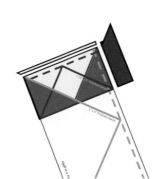

3. Turn patch around. Do not turn ruler. Trim off excess fabric on right and top.

4. Repeat with second half.

Sampler Two

1. Line up ruler's green lines on 45° sewn lines. Line up green dotted line with peak of triangle for ¼" seam allowance. Cut block in half to separate into two patches.

2. Trim excess fabric on all four sides. Turn mat around while trimming.

   ### Sampler Two
   Square to 3½" x 6½"
   Finished Geese is 3" x 6"

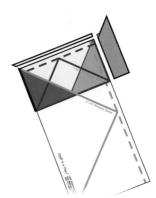

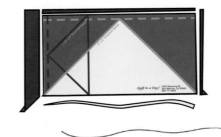

Making Center Squares

1. Sew red and green strips right sides together. Press seam toward green.

   Sampler One
   2" x 9" strips

   Sampler Two
   3½" x 15" strips

   Four Block Wallhanging
   2" x 26" strips

2. Square left end. Cut into pieces.

   Sampler One
   (4) 2" pieces

   Sampler Two
   (4) 3½" pieces

   Four Block Wallhanging
   (12) 2" pieces

2"
*Sampler One
and Four Block*

3½"
Sampler Two

3. Assembly-line sew pieces to red strip.

   Sampler One
   (1) 2" x 15"

   Sampler Two
   (2) 3½" x 15"

   Four Block Wallhanging
   (2) 2" strips

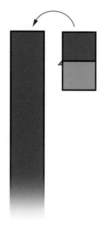

4. Cut apart between blocks.

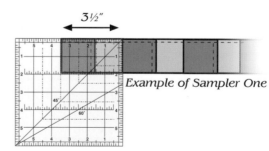

3½"

Example of Sampler One

5. Set seam with red strip on top, open, and press toward red. Measure square.

   Sampler One
   3½" square

   Sampler Two
   6½" square

   Four Block Wallhanging
   3½" square

Assembling Flowers

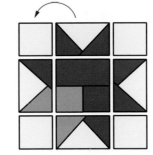

1. Lay out flower petals, center square, and Background corner squares.

Sampler One	**Sampler Two**
(16) 2" corner squares	(16) 3½" corner squares
Four are extra for a Bonus Block.	*Four are extra for a Bonus Block.*

   Four Block Wallhanging
   (48) 2" corner squares

Sampler One and Two: Make Four
Wallhanging: Make Twelve

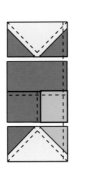

2. Flip middle vertical row right sides together to left vertical row.

3. Assembly-line sew. Do not clip connecting threads.

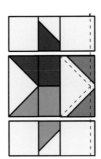

4. Flip remaining vertical row right sides together to middle vertical row. Assembly-line sew.

5. Clip apart every third patch, and stack.

6. Sew remaining rows, locking petal and center square seams. Push seams away from petals on top, and toward center underneath.

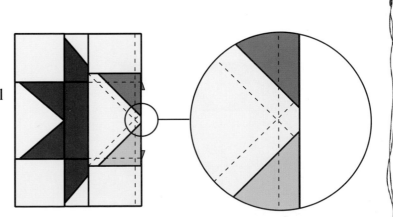

Peony

7. Press last sewn seams toward center.

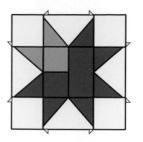

Sewing Block Together

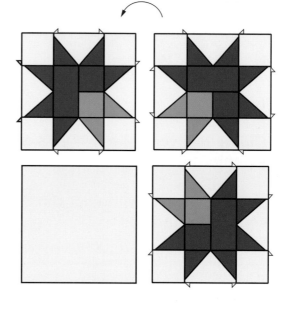

1. Lay out petals with Background square. Turn seams as illustrated so petals lock together.

   Sampler One
   (1) 6½" square

   Sampler Two
   (1) 12½" square

   Four Block Wallhanging
   (4) 6½" squares

2. Sew vertical seam.

3. Sew remaining row, pushing top seam down toward Background square and bottom seam up.

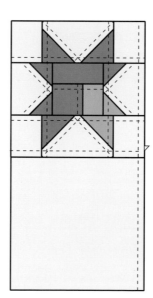

4. From wrong side, press last seam to left.

   Optional: Sew all four into one block and skip adding bias stems.

136

Cutting Bias Stems

1. Line up 45° line on 6" x 24" ruler with left edge of green fabric and cut. *Corner piece of fabric can be used.*

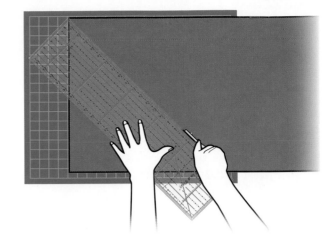

2. Move ruler over, and line designated bias strip width with diagonal edge. Cut bias strips.

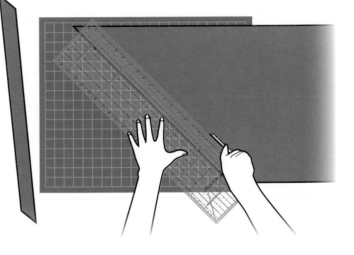

Sampler One
Curved Stem
(1) 1" x 11"
Center Stem
(1) 1¼" x 12"

Sampler Two
Curved Stem
(1) 1⅛" x 20"
Center Stem
(1) 1¼" x 24"

Four Block Wallhanging
Curved Stem
(4) 1" x 11"
Center Stem
(4) 1¼" x 12"

3. Pin one end of narrower bias strip for Curved Stem to pressing mat. Press bias strip in thirds lengthwise, wrong sides together.

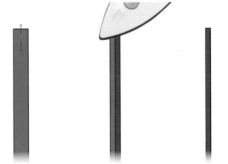

Place wrong side up.   Fold one third in and press.   Fold second third in and press.

Making Curved Stem

1. Remove ½" of stitches on three marked spots with seam ripper.

The ends of Stems are tucked in and hidden in these "holes".

2. Find Curved Stem pattern in back of book, and cut out.

3. Place pattern on Peony block, matching 90° angle on pattern with seams on block. Lightly trace curve with pencil or disappearing pen.

    Make sure to leave space between line and green petals.

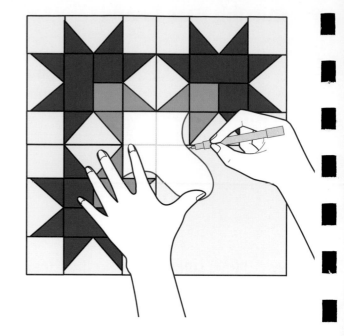

4. On right top side of marked line, tuck ½" of pressed bias strip into opened seam allowance. *Strip slides in same direction as seam.*

5. Line up folded bias edge with marked curved line. Carefully fingerpress bias strip flat, and pin in place. A little tuck at bottom of curve can be covered later with Center Stem.

6. At opposite end, trim ½" extra bias strip, and tuck into seam allowance. *Strip slides in fighting seam. Fold strip to match seam.*

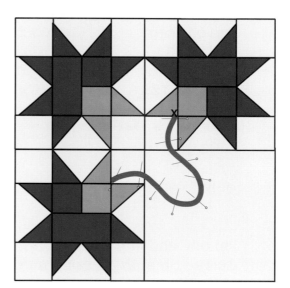

7. Hand applique inside edge of curve in place with matching thread. To keep thread from tangling, run regular thread through Thread Heaven® thread conditioner, or use waxed thread.

8. Remove pins and steam press in place.

9. Hand applique outside curve and tucked ends.

    Push threaded needle through fold from wrong side. Pull needle completely through fold. Push needle through Background next to place where needle came out. Move forward on underneath side of Background ⅟₁₆" to ⅛" and repeat stitch.

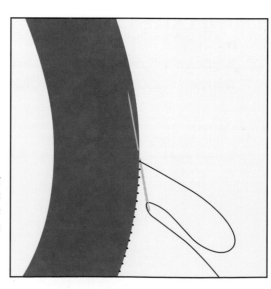

138

Making Center Stem

1. Press Center Stem bias strip in half lengthwise wrong sides together.

   Sampler One   **Sampler Two**
   (1) 1¼" x 12"   (1) 1¼" x 24" strip

   Four Block Wallhanging
   (4) 1¼" x 12"

2. Place pin on one end of bias strip ¼" in from raw edge. Pin to "V" in Peony.

3. Pin Center Stem from top to bottom, curving bias strip as you pin, and covering Curved Stem.

4. Machine sew ¼" seam from raw edge, beginning at bottom of Center Stem, and sewing toward top. Stop at pin.

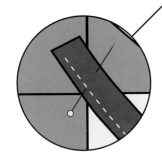

5. Press folded edge over seam. Tuck bias end in seam. Pin in place.

6. Hand applique edge in place.

7. Trim bottom of Stem to match block.

Making Leaves

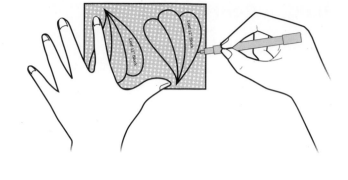

1.   Find Patterns on large sheet in back of book.

2.   Trace two mirror image Leaves on smooth side of non-woven fusible interfacing with permanent marking pen. Include center markings.

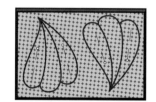

3.   Place rough, fusible side of interfacing against right side of Leaf fabric. Pin.

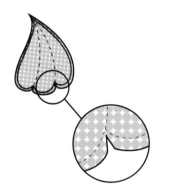

4.   With matching thread and 20 stitches per inch, or 1.8 on computerized machines, **sew on outside drawn lines only**.

5.   Trim seams to ⅛". Clip inside curves.

Turning Applique

1.   Cut small opening in center of interfacing. Insert straw into hole. Push straw against fabric.

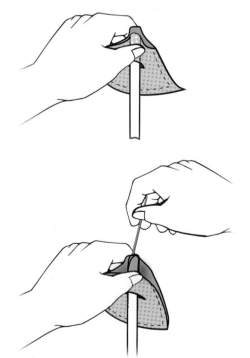

2.   Place ball of ball point bodkin on fabric stretched over straw. Gently push fabric into straw about 1" with bodkin to start turning Leaf. Do not try to push applique through straw and out other end.

3. Remove straw and bodkin. Insert straw in second half, and turn right side out.

4. Run bodkin around inside edge, pushing out seams.

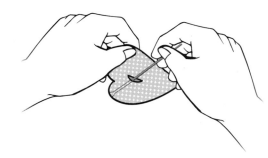

5. From right side, push fabric over interfacing edge with wooden iron.

6. Cut 100% cotton batting same size as Leaves. Insert batting though opening with hemostat.

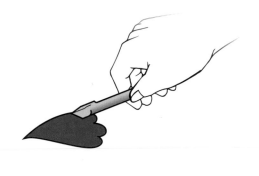

7. From wrong side, stitch on lines with matching thread.

8. Arrange Leaves on block, and steam press in place.

9. Hand or machine stitch around outside edges of Leaves.

Peony and Vine Wallhanging

Pieced by Eleanor Burns
Quilted by Carol Selepec
42" x 42"

Background 2 yds

Side Triangles	(1) 18½" square
Corner Triangles	(2) 10" squares
Center Square	(1) 12½" square
Border	(5) 5" strips

Blocks
(2) 4½" strips cut into
    (12) 4½" squares
(3) 2" strips cut into
    (48) 2" squares
(1) 6½" strip cut into
    (4) 6½" squares

Red 1⅛ yds

Petals
(2) 6" strips cut into
    (9) 6" squares
(3) 2" strips

Vine Buds
(1) 1¾" strip cut into
    (16) 1¾" squares

Binding
(5) 3" strips

Green 1¼ yds

Stems and Vine
(See page 137 for cutting bias.)
(1) 16" strip cut into
    (4) 1" x 11" bias strips
      for Curved Stem
    (4) 1¼" x 12" bias strips
      for Center Stem
    (7) 1¼" x 22" bias strips
      for Vine

Petals
(1) 6" strip cut into
    (3) 6" squares
(1) 2" strip

Leaves and Buds
(12) 3½" x 7½" pieces

Non-woven Fusible Interfacing ⅓ yd
(12) 3½" x 7½" pieces

Batting
48" x 48"

Backing
2¾ yds

Four Block Peony Wallhanging

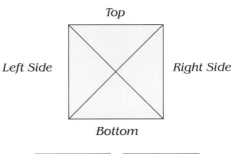

18½" Background Square

Top

Left Side   Right Side

Bottom

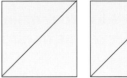

1. Make four 12" Peony blocks following instructions beginning on page 130.

2. Cut 18½" Background square into fourths on both diagonals for Side Triangles. Place as directed.

3. Cut two 10" Background squares in half on one diagonal for Corner Triangles.

4. Lay out four Peony blocks with 12½" Center Square, and Side and Corner Triangles.

5. Sew one diagonal row together at a time, with Triangles on bottom. Press seams toward Center Square and Triangles.

6. Trim tips from Triangles.

7. Sew rows together.

8. Find center on Corner Triangles and pin to center on Peony. Sew Corner Triangles.

9. If necessary, straighten outside edges without removing ¼" seam allowance.

10. Measure, pin, and sew 5" Borders to two opposite sides.

11. Press Border seams toward Border.

12. Sew Borders to two remaining sides. Press Border seams toward Border.

Making Vine Border

1. Sew bias 1¼" x 22" Vine strips into one long strip approximately 140" long.

2. Press in half lengthwise wrong sides together.

3. Cut out Vine pattern from back of book and tape together.

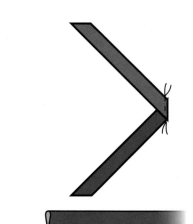

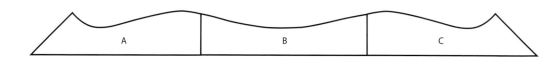

4. Line up Vine pattern with outside edge of Border strip. Trace inside scallop edge with pencil or disappearing pen on all four sides.

5. Place raw edges of folded bias strip on inside edge of line. Place folded edge toward inside. Leave 4" of Vine loose.

6. Use needle down position on your machine. Working in short sections ahead of needle, gently pull bias strip to curve and then sew ¼" seam. Ease on inside curves. Hold taut on outside curves.

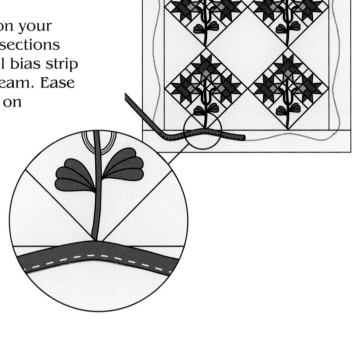

7. Stop stitching 4" from where ends will overlap.

8. Line up two ends. Trim excess with ½" overlap.

9. Open up folded ends and pin right sides together. Sew a ¼" seam. Continue sewing bias strip to Wallhanging.

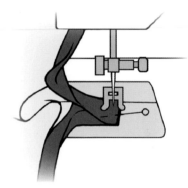

10. Fold strip back over raw edge. Gently steam press Vine flat.

11. Stitch in place by machine or hand.

   Machine Stitch: *Select blind hem stitch. Set stitch length to 1.0, and stitch width to 2.0. Place invisible thread on top, and loosen top tension. Place thread matching Background in bobbin. Stitch around loose edge, catching Vine with "bite" of blind hem stitch.*

   Hand Stitch: *Use applique stitch. See page 138.*

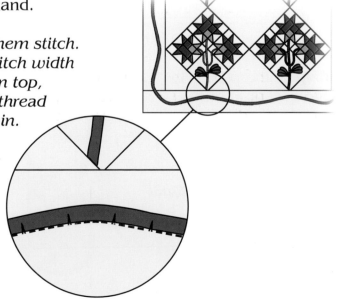

Folding Buds

1. Fold 1¾" red squares wrong sides together on the diagonal. Press.

2. Fold in ends. Press.

3. Run a gathering stitch across bottom edge, pull up, and knot.

Making Leaves and Bud Stems

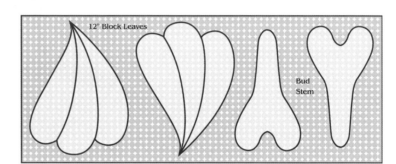

1. Trace eight sets of Leaves and Buds on smooth side of 3" x 7½" piece fusible interfacing.

2. Place fusible side of interfacing against right side of 3" x 7½" green fabric.

3. Follow instructions on pages 140-141.

Placing Buds and Leaves on Vine

1. Place four sets of Buds and Leaves on each side of Wallhanging.

2. Tuck Buds under Bud Stems.

3. Fuse in place with steam iron.

4. Handstitch through Bud to anchor in place.

5. Handstitch around Bud Stem and Leaves.

6. Turn to *Layering Your Quilt* on page 224.

Eleanor Burns
14" x 16½"

Teresa Varnes
24" x 27"

BONUS PILLOW
from Sampler One

One 6½" Extra Peony block

Stems and Leaves ⅛ yd
(1) 1¼" x 6" bias strip
(1) 3½" x 5"

**Non-woven Fusible
Interfacing ⅛ yd**
(1) 3½" x 5"

Side Triangles ¼ yd
(1) 5¼" square
    Cut on one diagonal
(1) 7" square
    Cut on one diagonal

Pillow ½ yd
(2) 15" x 21¼"
Matching Thread

Rickrack ½" wide
1 yd
Matching Thread

Mixed Buttons
(6) ¾"

Pillow Form 14" Square

BONUS WALLHANGING
from Sampler Two

One 12½" Extra Peony block

Stems and Leaves ¼ yd
(1) 1¼" x 12" bias strip
(1) 5" x 7½"

**Non-woven Fusible
Interfacing ¼ yd**
(1) 5" x 7½"

Side Triangles ⅜ yd
(1) 9½" square
    Cut on one diagonal
(1) 12½" square
    Cut on one diagonal

Folded Border ⅛ yd
(2) 1¼" strips

Border ⅜ yd
(3) 4" strips

Binding ⅓ yd
(3) 3" strips

Backing ¾ yd

Batting 30" x 33"

Adding Side Triangles

1. Place triangle from smaller square on top left, and triangle from larger square on bottom right with extra peony block.

6½" Peony Block	**12½" Peony Block**
Small 5¼" square	Small 9½" square
Large 7" square	Large 12½" square

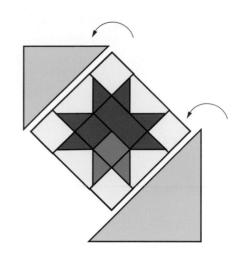

2. Center top left triangle with ⅜" tips hanging over on both ends. Flip right sides together, and sew.

3. Place bottom right triangle with ⅜" tip hanging over on top end only. Flip right sides together, and sew.

4. Press seams toward triangles.

5. Trim triangles even with block.

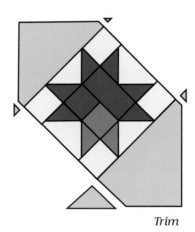

Trim

6. Center remaining two triangles on block, flip right sides together, and sew.

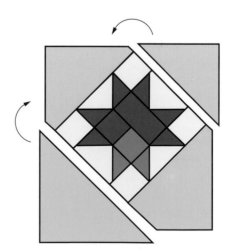

7. Press seams toward triangles.

8. Square rectangle with 6½" block to approximately 9" x 10½".

   Square rectangle with 12½" block to approximately 17½" x 20½".

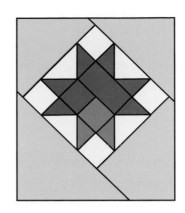

9. Unsew ½" of stitches in seam at spot marked with X.

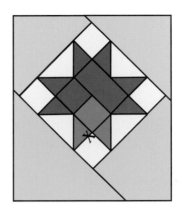

10. Sew bias Stem to Peony following directions on page 139.

11. Make two Leaves and sew to block following directions on pages 140-141.

Finishing Wallhanging

1. Sew Folded Border to Wallhanging following directions on page 98.

2. Turn to *Adding Borders* on page 220.

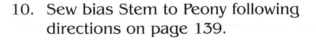

Finishing Pillow

1. Find Curved Pattern for Peony Bonus Pillow on large sheet in back of book and cut out.

2. Place pattern on patchwork, and round corners.

3. Line up edge of rickrack with curved raw edge, and sew ¼" from edge.

4. Turn under rickrack.

5. Find centers on one pillow piece and patchwork. Pin patchwork in place.

6. Baste top ⅛" from edge.

7. With thread matching rickrack, stitch in the ditch through rickrack.

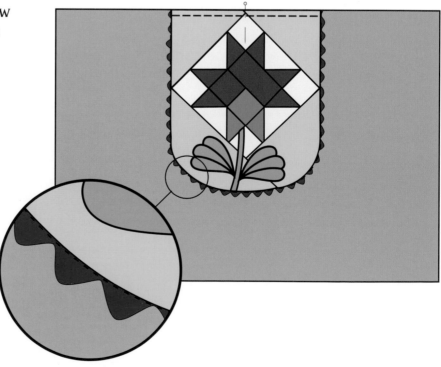

8. Press four 15" sides under ⅜", and edgestitch with matching thread.

9. Clip notches 2" from outside edges, and draw lines 4" in from outside edges on both pieces.

10. Place pieces right sides together with Front on the top. Match raw edges, and hemmed edges.

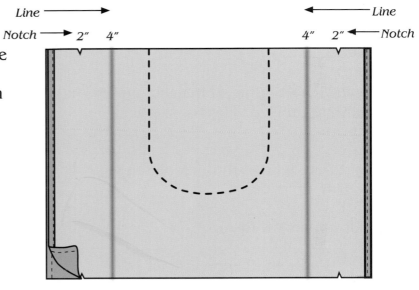

11. To make a clean inside finish, fold both pieces together on 2" notch and bring folded edgestitch edges to 4" line. Pin.

12. Repeat on four corners.

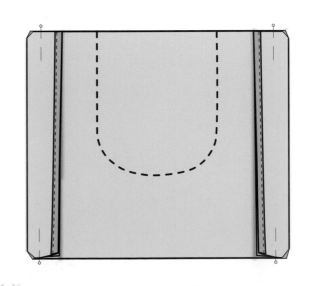

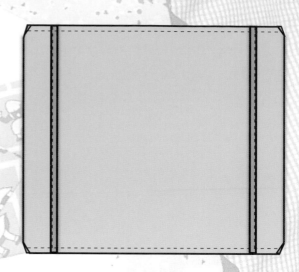

13. Sew both sides with ¼" seam. Remove pins.

14. Turn right side out.

15. From wrong side, line up folds with 4" lines.

16. Edgestitch with thread matching pillow, following previous lines of stitching. Press.

17. Sew three buttons through all thickness on one side.

18. Stuff with pillow form.

19. Sew three buttons on remaining side.

Remembering the 1930's

1930 More than 1,300 American Banks fail, unemployment exceeds 4 million as Depression sinks

1931 The Star Spangled Banner becomes the national anthem

1932 Kodak introduces 8 mm film for home movies

1933 Phonograph records go stereo

1934 Infamous bank robbers, Clyde Barrow and Bonnie Parker are killed by police in Louisiana

1935 Benny Goodman and band usher in the Swing Era

1936 The first Bob's Big Boy opens

1937 First Social Security checks distributed

1938 Congress establishes a minimum wage – 25 cents an hour

1939 "Gone With the Wind" premieres in Atlanta

Lemon Raisin Scones

4 cups flour
1/2 cup sugar
4 teaspoonfuls baking powder
3/4 teaspoonful salt
3/4 cup butter
1 cup raisins
1 cup milk
2 eggs
1 tablespoonful vanilla
1 tablespoonful grated lemon peel

In large bowl mix flour, sugar, baking powder, and salt. Cut butter in with pastry blender. Add raisins. In another bowl, whisk milk, eggs, vanilla, and fresh lemon peel together. Pour into flour. Combine with fork. Divide in three pieces. Pat each piece into a circle on a floured board. Sprinkle with coarse sugar. Cut in eight pieces. Put pieces on well-greased cookie sheet. Bake at 400 degrees for 15 to 20 minutes.

Pieced by Teresa Varnes
24" x 24"

For many, the neighborhood grocery offered a means of survival in very trying times. Many family-owned stores extended credit to regular customers, who paid their bills when they got money. Many couldn't pay. Folks couldn't brag that they "ate high off the hog", but one way or another, they ate!

𝒮tudents at our 2004 Block Party decided to gather signatures from celebrity quilters. This quilt is not finished yet because there are many more individuals that deserve their name on this quilt, preserved for posterity.

Friendship

Also known as

- Signature
- Celebrity

Sampler One
One 12" Block
Finished Size

Background
(16) 3½" squares

**Variety of
Medium Prints**
(32) 2½" squares

Sampler Two
Seven 6" Blocks
Finished Size

Background
(28) 3½" squares

**Variety of
Medium Prints**
(56) 2½" squares

Supplies

❏ Permanent
   Marking Pen

❏ 6" Square Up Ruler

❏ 6" x 12" Ruler

❏ Easy Angler
   (Optional)

Making 3½" Squares

1. Draw diagonal line on wrong side of 2½" prints with permanent marking pen.

   Optional: Install the Angler on your sewing machine to save time drawing lines. Match the corner of the 2½" square with the angled diagonal line, and sew.

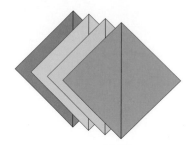

2. Place 2½" print right sides together to 3½" Background square. Line up outside edges.

3. Hold threads to get started. Assembly-line sew on right side of diagonal line.

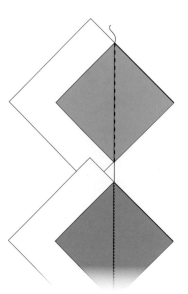

4. Trim ¼" from diagonal line.

5. Clip connecting threads.

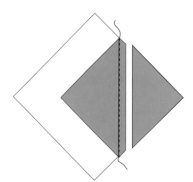

6. Set seam, open, and press toward print.

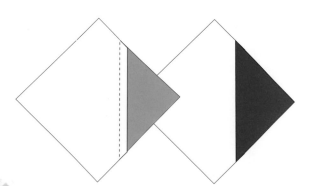

7. Place different print on opposite side of 3½" Background square, right sides together. Line up outside edges.

8. Assembly-line sew on right side of diagonal line.

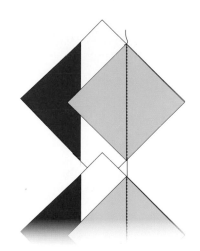

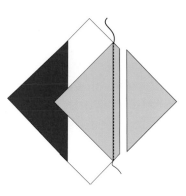

9. Trim ¼" from diagonal line. Clip connecting threads.

10. Set seam, open, and press toward print.

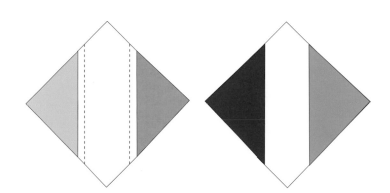

Making 6½" Squares

1. Lay out sets of four 3½" squares. Carefully mix prints so same colors or fabrics are not next to each other.

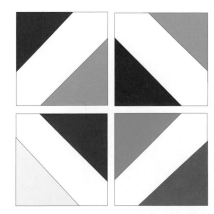

Sampler One
Four Sets

Sampler Two
Seven Sets

2.	If they are signed, arrange them with signatures up.

3.	On two opposite blocks, repress seams toward Background so seams lock together.

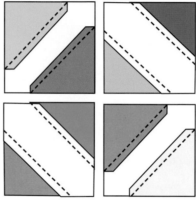

Repress seams toward Background.

Repress seams toward Background.

4.	Flip right vertical row to left vertical row, right sides together.

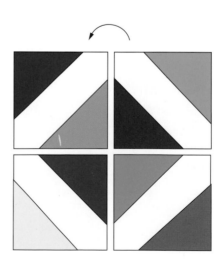

5. Assembly-line sew with scant ¼" seam, locking seams.

6. Clip apart every two blocks.

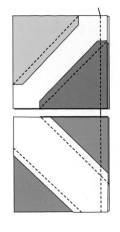

Sew with scant ¼" seam.

7. Assembly-line sew remaining seam. Lock seams, push top seam up, and underneath seam down.

8. Clip connecting thread.

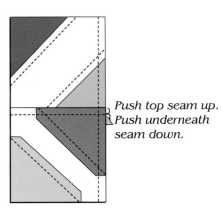

Push top seam up. Push underneath seam down.

Push top vertical seam to right.

9. Place block wrong side up. Push top vertical seam to right, and bottom vertical seam to left. Center stitches pop open, forming a small four-patch.

10. Flatten four-patch with finger.

11. Press seams clockwise around four-patch.

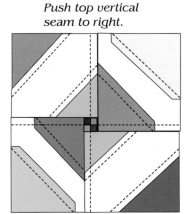

Push bottom vertical seam to left.

12. Seven 6½" blocks for Sampler Two are complete. Set aside.

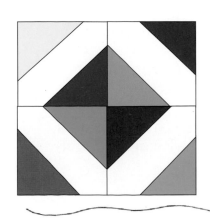

Making 12½" Block for Sampler One

1. Lay out four 6½" blocks.

2. Flip right vertical row to left vertical row, right sides together. Assembly-line sew, locking seams.

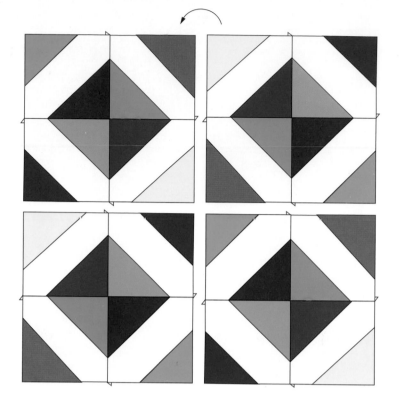

Push top vertical seam to right.

3. Assembly-line sew remaining seam. Lock seams, push top seam up, and underneath seam down.

4. Clip connecting thread. Place block wrong side up. Push top vertical seam to right, and bottom vertical seam to left. Center stitches pop open, forming a small four-patch.

5. Flatten center into four-patch.

6. Press just sewn seams clockwise around four-patch.

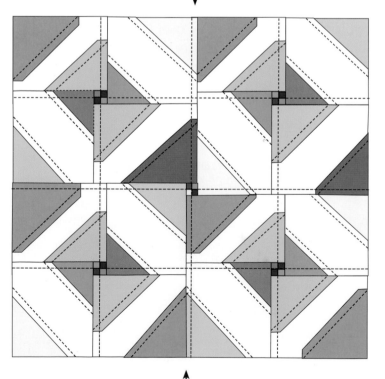

Push bottom vertical seam to left.

Friendship Wallhanging

*Pieced and Quilted
by Sue Bouchard
20" x 28"*

Choose this layout for Friendship blocks if you don't want to repress or match seams. This little quilt was signed by everyone who attended the bridal shower for Sue's niece, Lissy Clark. The quilt's pansy floral border was chosen to coordinate with her Pansy Party theme. Along with their signatures, guests wrote their relationship to the bride.

Friendship Pillow

Teresa made a one block pillow for Nobuko Depew as a special "We'll Miss You" present, and had key people in the company sign the remembrance blocks.

*Pieced and Quilted
by Teresa Varnes
18" x 18"*

Pieced by Teresa Varnes
Quilted by Carol Selepec
94" x 108"

In the 1930's, area churches held singing conventions. The farmers tried to have the revival before spring planting and after crops were "laid by" for the summer. That way the wagons could be filled with church members going to and from the revivals.

Methodist churches were known for their "quilting bees." Ladies would sit down to a frame, and stitch on the same quilt together. When the quilt was finished, it was raffled off, with the proceeds going to the church. All the ladies would bring a dessert, and during rest periods, they enjoyed these home-made goodies.

A particular curved quilting pattern was named the Baptist quilting stitch, from ladies sitting elbow to elbow at the quilting frame, and quilting as far as they could reach.

Christian Cross

Also known as

• Chimney Sweep

There are yardage charts and instructions for two sizes of blocks, and five quilts. Turn to page 172 for quilt instructions.

Sampler One (page 164)
One 12" Block Finished Size

Background
(1) 3" strip cut into
    (12) 3" x 2⅝"
    (2) 3" squares

Medium
(1) 2⅝" strip cut into
    (1) 2⅝" x 6⅞"
    (2) 2⅝" squares

Dark
(2) 2⅝" strips cut into
    (6) 2⅝" x 4⅝"
    (2) 2⅝" x 6⅞"
    (2) 2⅝" squares

Sampler Two (page 165)
Four 9" Blocks Finished Size

Background
(1) 3" strip cut into
    (8) 3" squares
(3) 2½" strips cut in half

Medium
(1) 5¼" x 12" strip
(1) 2⅛" half strip

Dark
(1) 5¼" half strip
(2) 3¾" strips cut into
    (2) 3¾" half strips
    (2) 3¾" x 12" strips
(1) 2⅛" half strip

Supplies

❏ 6" x 24" Ruler

❏ 12½" Square Up Ruler

❏ 9½" Square Up Ruler for Sampler Two (Optional)

Color variation on Christian Cross

163

Making One 12½" Block
for Sampler One

Row One

1. Lay out Background and Dark pieces. Stack two on top of each other. Assembly-line sew two rows together.

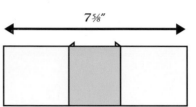

3" x 2⅝"   *2⅝"*   *3" x 2⅝"*
Background   *Dark*   *Background*

7⅝"

2. Press seams toward Dark.

3. Check length of row.

Row Two

1. Lay out Background and Dark pieces. Stack two on top of each other. Assembly-line sew two rows together.

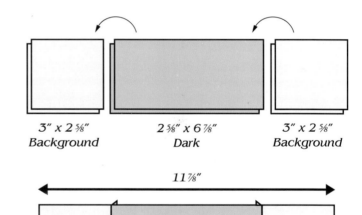

3" x 2⅝"   *2⅝" x 6⅞"*   *3" x 2⅝"*
Background   *Dark*   *Background*

11⅞"

2. Press seams toward Dark.

3. Check length of row.

Row Three

1. Lay out these pieces. Stack two on top of each other. Assembly-line sew two rows together.

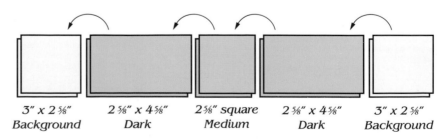

3" x 2⅝"   *2⅝" x 4⅝"*   *2⅝" square*   *2⅝" x 4⅝"*   *3" x 2⅝"*
Background   *Dark*   *Medium*   *Dark*   *Background*

2. Press seams toward Dark.

3. Check length of row.

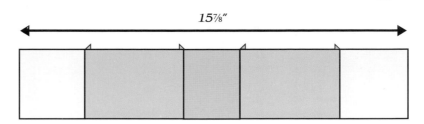

15⅞"

Row Four

1. Lay out Dark and Medium pieces. Sew one row together.

2. Press seams toward Dark.

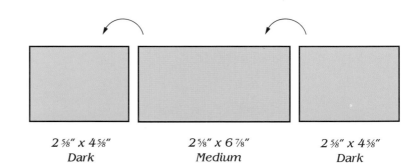

2 ⅝" x 4⅝"
Dark

2 ⅝" x 6⅞"
Medium

2 ⅝" x 4⅝"
Dark

3. Check length of row.

4. Turn to *Sewing Block Together*, page 168.

15⅛"

Making Four 9½" Blocks for Sampler Two

Sew with a ⁵⁄₁₆" seam allowance which is a little wider than ¼".

Measure your seam against this measurement:

⁵⁄₁₆"

Row One

1. Lay out Background and Dark strips. Line up cut edges at top. Sew strips together.

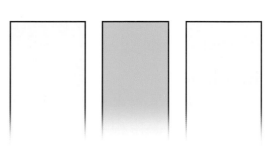

2 ½" half strip
Background

2 ⅛" half
strip Dark

2 ½" half strip
Background

2. Press seams toward Dark.

3. Check length.

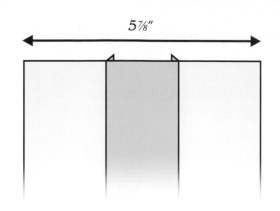

5⅞"

4. Cut into (8) 2⅛" sections.

Option: Layer cut all sections after sewing and pressing is completed.

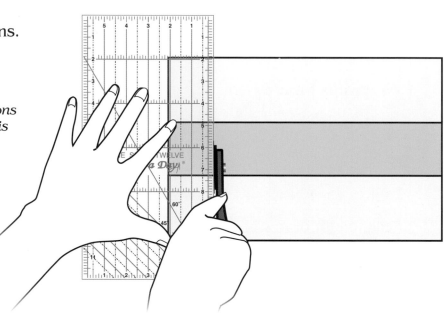

Row Two

1. Lay out Background and Dark strips. Sew strips together.

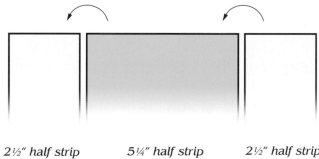

2½" half strip
Background

5¼" half strip
Dark

2½" half strip
Background

2. Press seams toward Dark.

3. Check length.

4. Cut into (8) 2⅛" sections.

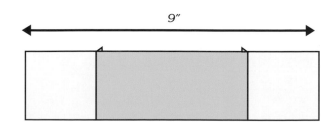

9"

166

Row Three

1. Lay out these strips. Sew strips together.

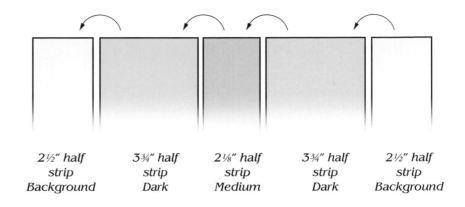

2½" half strip Background *3¾" half strip Dark* *2⅛" half strip Medium* *3¾" half strip Dark* *2½" half strip Background*

2. Press seams toward Dark.

3. Check length.

4. Cut into (8) 2⅛" sections.

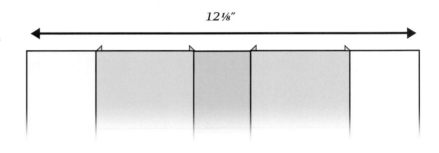

12⅛"

Row Four

1. Lay out Dark and Medium strips. Sew strips together.

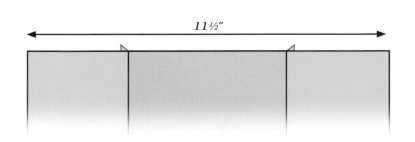

3¾" x 12" Dark *5¼" x 12" Medium* *3¾" x 12" Dark*

2. Press seams toward Dark.

3. Check length.

4. Cut into (4) 2⅛" sections.

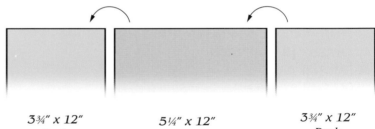

11½"

Sewing Block Together

1. Fold Row Four and Row Three in half and press.

2. Lay out four rows.
    Sampler Two: Stack four in each row.

3. Sew Row Three to Row Four, matching center crease lines.

4. Sew Row Two to Row Three. From wrong side, line up seams on Row Two with seams on Row Four.

5. Sew Row One to Row Two. From wrong side, line up seams on Row One with seams on Row Three.

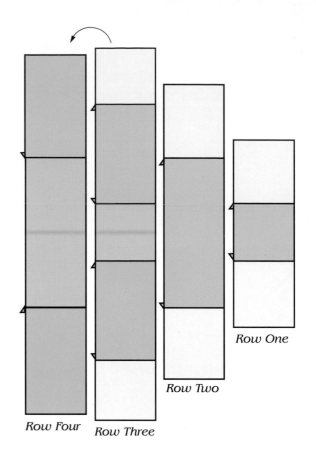

Row One

Row Two

Row Four   Row Three

6. From wrong side, press seams away from center Row Four. From right side, press out any folds.

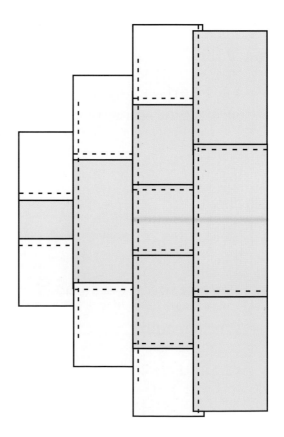

7. Turn and sew remaining rows to center, lining up centers and seams.

8. From wrong side, press seams away from center Row Four.

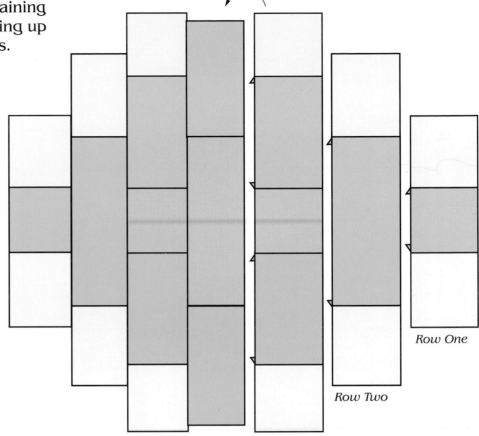

Row One

Row Two

Row Three

9. Trim two outside edges.

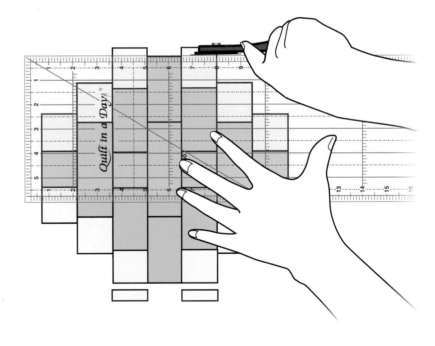

10. Cut two 3" Background squares per block in half on one diagonal. Fold in half and fingerpress.

11. Fold outside edges of block in half and fingerpress.

12. Center and sew triangles to four corners of block.

13. Press seams toward Background Triangle.

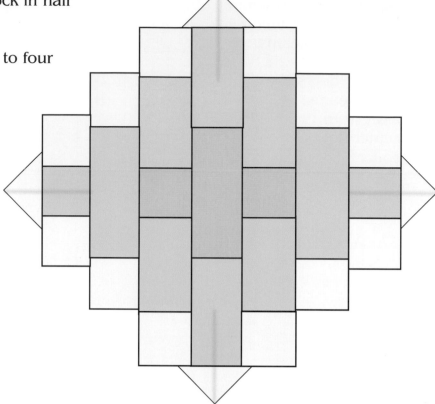

Squaring Up Sampler One 12½" Block

1. With hera marker, chalk, or disappearing pen, lightly draw diagonal lines down center of block.

2. Place 12½" Square Up Ruler with diagonal line down center of Row Four. Place ruler's 6¼" center mark on block.

3. Slide ruler around so you have at least an extra ¼" Background from tips.

4. Trim on all four sides.

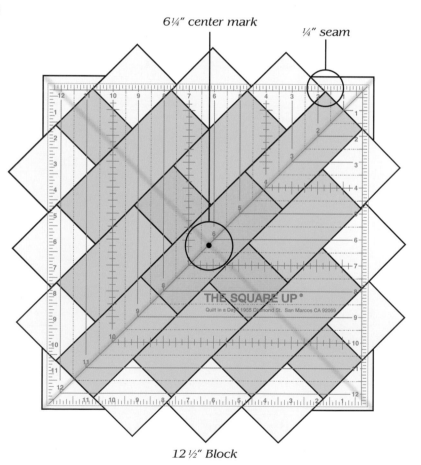

6¼" center mark

¼" seam

12½" Block

Depending on your seam allowance, the blocks may "float" with extra Background around the outside edges.

Squaring Up Sampler Two
Four 9½" Blocks

If 9½" Square Up Ruler is available, center on block and trim four sides. Directions are written for 12½" Square Up Ruler.

1. With hera marker, chalk, or disappearing pen, lightly draw diagonal lines down center of block.

2. Place 12½" Square Up Ruler with diagonal line down center of Row Four. Place 4¾" center mark on block.

3. Slide ruler around so you have at least an extra ¼" Background from tips.

4. Trim right side and across top.

5. Turn block halfway around so untrimmed edges are on top and right. Do not turn ruler.

6. Place ruler with diagonal line down center of Row Four. Place 9½" squaring lines on just cut edges, and 4¾" on center mark.

7. Trim right side and across top.

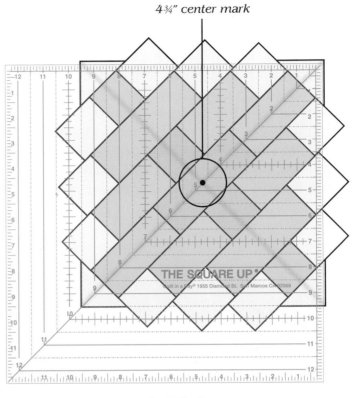

4¾" center mark

9½" Block

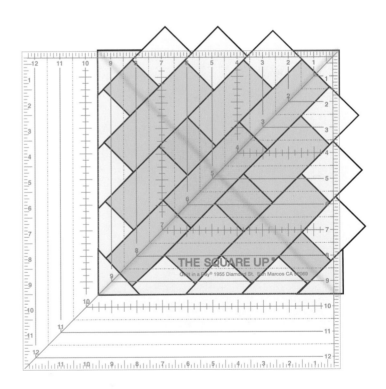

Christian Cross Quilts

Selecting Fabric

Select one Background, and pairs of medium and dark prints that coordinate with each other for blocks. Each size quilt lists the number of pairs to purchase. For an old fashioned looking quilt, vary the scales of the prints, including large, medium, and small scale as well as plaids and polka dots.

Select a small scale medium that reads solid from a distance for Side and Corner Triangles, and an additional medium and dark of your favorite prints for Borders. Check the width of your fabrics. It is best to select fabrics approximately 44" in width.

Cutting Medium and Dark Half Strips for Blocks

Cut ¼ and ⅓ yd pieces in half on fold first so two pieces are approximately 22" wide. Cut half strips following cutting charts. Do not trim off selvage edges.

Pieced by Teresa Varnes
Quilted by Carol Selepec
94" x 108"

In this queen, ten sets of medium and dark fabrics were selected. Five blocks from each set were assembly-line sewn for a total of fifty blocks.

172

*Pieced by Eleanor Burns
Quilted by Amie Potter
39" x 39"*

*F*or a Wallhanging, select a Background, one medium, and one dark print for five blocks. Use same medium for Side and Corner triangles, and Binding if you choose. Purchase additional dark fabric for the 4" Border.

*Pieced by Teresa Varnes
Quilted by Amie Potter
39" x 39"*

*I*n this wallhanging, Side Triangles were cut from one fabric, and Corner Triangles were cut from a second fabric.

Christian Cross Yardage Charts

Finished Block Size 9" square	Wallhanging 5 Blocks 38" x 38"	Lap 18 Blocks 54" x 68"

One Background
Blocks
	1½ yds
	    (3) 2½" strips cut into
	        (6) 2½" half strips
	    (1) 3" strip cut into
	        (10) 3" squares
		2¼ yds
		    (12) 2½" strips cut into
		        (24) 2½" half strips
		    (4) 3" strips cut into
		        (36) 3" squares

Lattice	(2) 2" strips cut into
	    (8) 2" x 9½"
	(3) 2" strips
		(6) 2" strips cut into
		    (24) 2" x 9½"
		(7) 2" strips

Different Darks
Blocks
	(1) ⅓ yd piece
	    Cut each into
	(1) 2⅛" half strip
	(1) 5¼" half strip
	(2) 3¾" half strips
	(2) 3¾" x 12"
		(4) ⅓ yd pieces
		    Cut each into
		(1) 2⅛" half strip
		(1) 5¼" half strip
		(2) 3¾" half strips
		(2) 3¾" x 12"

Different Mediums
Blocks
	(1) ¼ yd piece
	    Cut each into
	(1) 5¼" x 12"
	(1) 2⅛" half strip
		(4) ¼ yd pieces
		    Cut each into
		(1) 5¼" x 12"
		(1) 2⅛" half strip

One Medium Side Triangles Corner Triangles	½ yd (1) 16½" square (2) 10" squares	1 yd (3) 16½" squares (2) 10" squares
First Border	½ yd (4) 4" strips	⅜ yd (6) 2" strips
Second Border		1⅛ yds (7) 5" strips
Third Border		
Binding	⅜ yd (4) 3" strips	⅔ yd (7) 3" strips
Backing	1¼ yds	4¼ yds
Batting	46" x 46"	62" x 76"

Twin 23 Blocks 65" x 95"	Full/Queen 50 Blocks 97" x 112"	King 85 Blocks 118" x 118"

2¾ yds
(15) 2½" strips cut into
  (30) 2½" half strips
(4) 3" strips cut into
  (46) 3" squares
 	
(9) 2" strips cut into
  (36) 2" x 9½"
(10) 2" strips
	4⅝ yds
	(30) 2½" strips cut into
	  (60) 2½" half strips
	(8) 3" strips cut into
	  (100) 3" squares
	
	(15) 2" strips cut into
	  (60) 2" x 9½"
	(17) 2" strips
		8 yds
		(51) 2½" strips cut into
		  (102) 2½" half strips
		(14) 3" strips cut into
		  (170) 3" squares
		
		(25) 2" strips cut into
		  (98) 2" x 9½"
		(26) 2" strips

(5) ⅓ yd pieces Cut each into (1) 2⅛" half strip (1) 5¼" half strip (2) 3¾" half strips (2) 3¾" x 12"	(10) ⅓ yd pieces Cut each into (1) 2⅛" half strip (1) 5¼" half strip (2) 3¾" half strips (2) 3¾" x 12"	(17) ⅓ yd pieces Cut each into (1) 2⅛" half strip (1) 5¼" half strip (2) 3¾" half strips (2) 3¾" x 12"
(5) ¼ yd pieces Cut each into (1) 5¼" x 12 (1) 2⅛" half strip	(10) ¼ yd pieces Cut each into (1) 5¼" x 12 (1) 2⅛" half strip	(17) ¼ yd pieces Cut each into (1) 5¼" x 12" (1) 2⅛" half strip
1⅓ yds (4) 16½" squares (2) 10" squares	1½ yds (5) 16½" squares (2) 10" squares	2 yds (6) 16½" squares (2) 10" squares
½ yd (7) 2" strips	⅝ yd (9) 2" strips	⅝ yd (10) 2" strips
¾ yd (7) 3½" strips	1 yd (9) 3½" strips	1⅛ yds (11) 3½" strips
1⅝ yds (9) 6" strips	1¾ yds (10) 6" strips	2 yds (11) 6" strips
⅞ yd (9) 3" strips	1 yd (10) 3" strips	1⅛ yds (12) 3" strips
6¼ yds	10½ yds	10½ yds
70" x 112"	104" x 120"	126" x 126"

Wallhanging

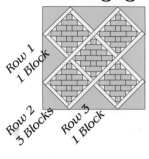

Row 1
1 Block

Row 2
3 Blocks

Row 3
1 Block

Lap

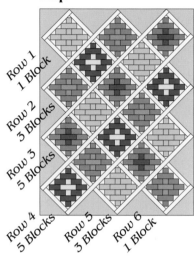

Row 1
1 Block

Row 2
3 Blocks

Row 3
5 Blocks

Row 4
5 Blocks

Row 5
3 Blocks

Row 6
1 Block

Full/Queen

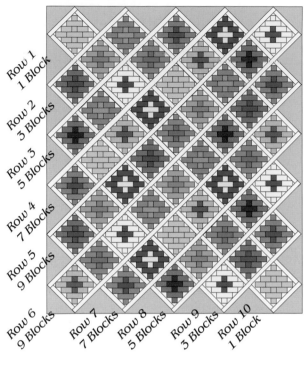

Row 1
1 Block

Row 2
3 Blocks

Row 3
5 Blocks

Row 4
7 Blocks

Row 5
9 Blocks

Row 6
9 Blocks

Row 7
7 Blocks

Row 8
5 Blocks

Row 9
3 Blocks

Row 10
1 Block

Twin

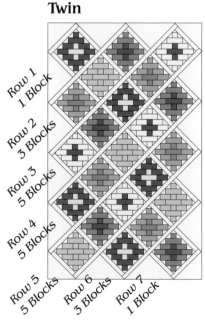

Row 1
1 Block

Row 2
3 Blocks

Row 3
5 Blocks

Row 4
5 Blocks

Row 5
5 Blocks

Row 6
3 Blocks

Row 7
1 Block

King

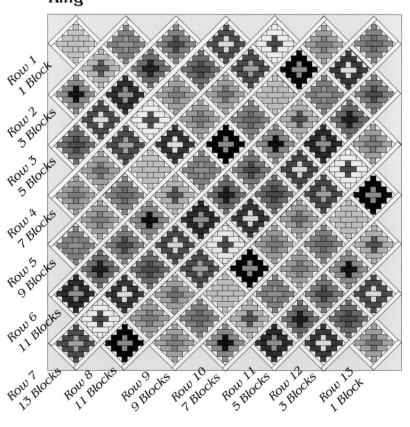

Row 1
1 Block

Row 2
3 Blocks

Row 3
5 Blocks

Row 4
7 Blocks

Row 5
9 Blocks

Row 6
11 Blocks

Row 7
13 Blocks

Row 8
11 Blocks

Row 9
9 Blocks

Row 10
7 Blocks

Row 11
5 Blocks

Row 12
3 Blocks

Row 13
1 Block

Making Blocks

1. From each pair of coordinated medium and dark prints, make **five** identical 9½" blocks. Sewing instructions begin on page 165.

Wallhanging	(1) set of five blocks
Lap	(4) sets of five blocks (two are extra)
Twin	(5) sets of five blocks (two are extra)
Full/Queen	(10) sets of five blocks
King	(17) sets of five blocks

2. Be economical when trimming selvage edges and cutting strips from each row to get total number of sections needed.

Row One	Cut (10) 2⅛" sections.
Row Two	Cut (10) 2⅛" sections
Row Three	Cut (10) 2⅛" sections
Row Four	Cut (5) 2⅛" sections

3. Lay out blocks in diagonal rows.

4. Stack blocks in diagonal rows from left to right, with left block on the top. Place a pin through row and label.

5. Stack each row with equal numbers of 2" x 9½" Lattice strips and blocks.

6. Flip block right sides together to Lattice and assembly-line sew.

7. Set seam with Lattice on top, open, and press toward Lattice.

8. Sew blocks together in diagonal rows.

9. Assembly-line sew Lattice to right side of blocks in all rows. Set seam with Lattice on top, open, and press toward Lattice.

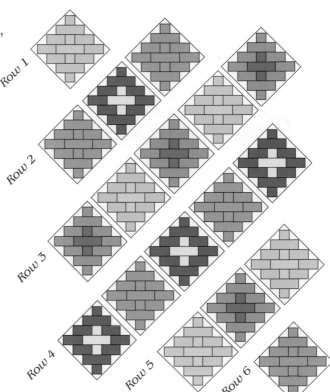

Lap Example

Row 1
Row 2
Row 3
Row 4
Row 5
Row 6

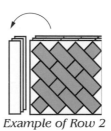

Example of Row 2

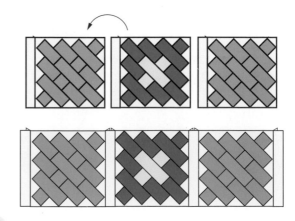

10. Piece 2" Lattice strips together, end to end. Clip connecting threads. Press seams open.

11. Lay out blocks in diagonal rows with Side Triangles. Lay out Lattice strips, including Lattice for Side Triangles as in Row 4. Cut Lattice slightly longer.

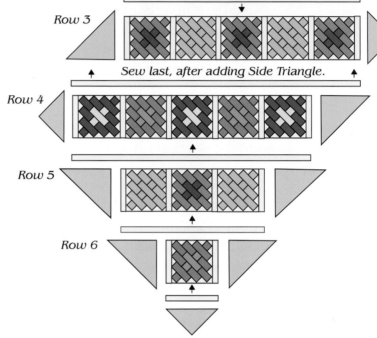

Lap

Row 1

Row 2

Row 3

Sew last, after adding Side Triangle.

12. Following arrows, sew Lattice to row first, and then sew Side Triangles to each row.

Row 4

13. Press seams toward Side Triangles and Lattice.

Row 5

Row 6

14. Sew rows together, lining up Lattice between blocks.

15. Sew Corner Triangles. Press seams toward Corners.

16. Square outside edges, leaving ¼" seam on all sides.

17. Turn to **Adding Borders** on page 220.

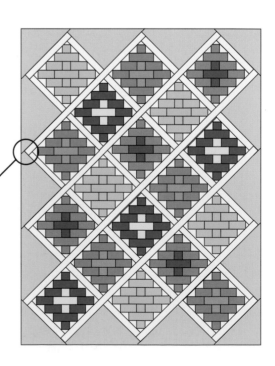

178

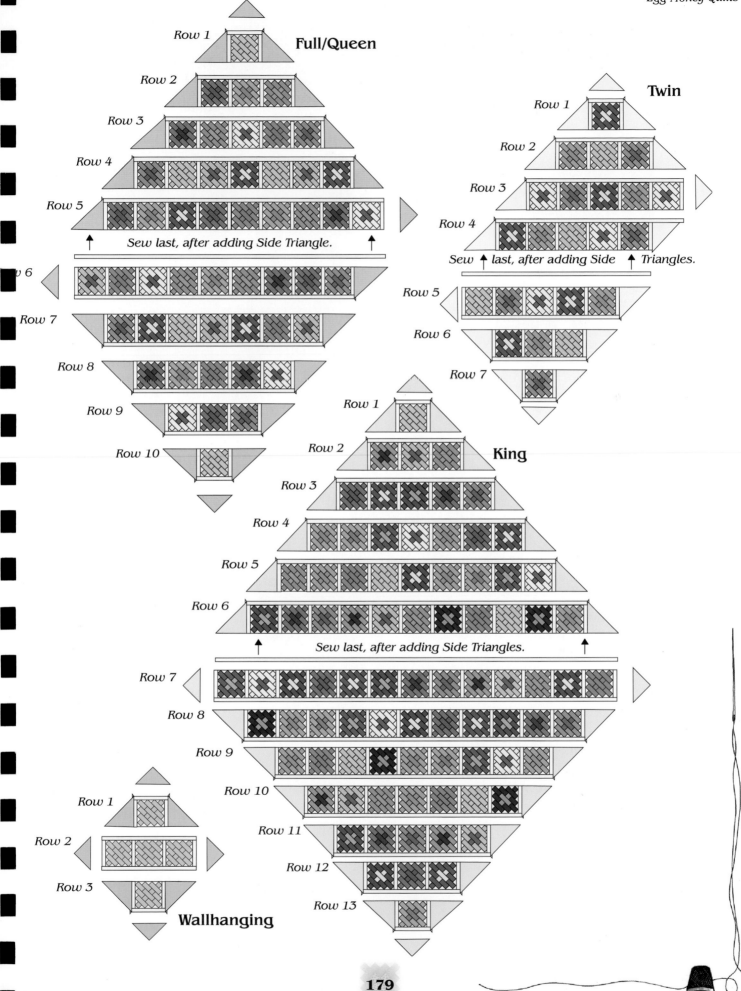

Full/Queen

Row 1
Row 2
Row 3
Row 4
Row 5

Sew last, after adding Side Triangle.

Row 6
Row 7
Row 8
Row 9
Row 10

Twin

Row 1
Row 2
Row 3
Row 4

Sew last, after adding Side Triangles.

Row 5
Row 6
Row 7

King

Row 1
Row 2
Row 3
Row 4
Row 5
Row 6

Sew last, after adding Side Triangles.

Row 7
Row 8
Row 9
Row 10
Row 11
Row 12
Row 13

Row 1
Row 2
Row 3

Wallhanging

*Antique Quilt from collection
of Eleanor Burns*

𝒩otice the extra embroidered protective piece of fabric sewn across the top of the quilt. It was often called "Grandpa's Whisker Cloth!" Perhaps this beautiful pink quilt wasn't for Grandpa at all, but Mother.

The worst of times brings out the best in people. Neighbors shared what little they had, often exchanging items from their small gardens — a cabbage for green beans, and carrots for tomatoes. Shortage drew many people closer together.

𝒯here are yardage charts and instructions for one block or five different sizes of quilts. Turn to pages 192-193 for quilt yardage.

Garden Walk

Also known as

- *Garden Patch*
- *Bird of Paradise*
- *Beggars Block*
- *Texas Block*
- *Fifty Four Forty or Fight*

Samplers One and Two
One 12" Block Finished Size
for each Sampler

Background
(1) 5" x 16"
(4) 2½" x 6"

First Flower
(2) 3" x 6"
(3) 2½" x 6"

Second Flower
(2) 3" x 6"
(3) 2½" x 6"

Supplies

❏ 6" x 12" Ruler

❏ Triangle in a
   Square Rulers
   or

❏ Template Plastic

❏ 6" x 8" Cutting Mat

This pattern uses Triangle in a Square Rulers from Quilt in a Day. If you do not own these rulers, make your own templates from patterns on page 195.

Cutting Background Triangles

1. Place 5" Background strips right side up. Place Triangle ruler on strip, **accurately lining up narrow part** of triangle with top of strip. The bottom is not as critical.

2. Cut Background triangles with rotary cutter, turning ruler with each cut.

Number of Triangles	
One Block	4
Wallhanging	16
Lap	48
Twin	60
Full/Queen	120
King	144

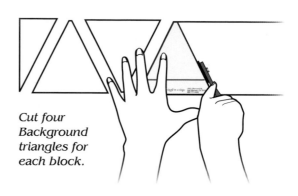

Cut four Background triangles for each block.

Cutting 3" x 6" Rectangles

1. Place pairs of 3" x 6" rectangles of same color **wrong sides together.** This step is essential for mirror image pieces.

Pairs of Rectangles of Each Color	
One Block	1
Wallhanging	4
Lap	12
Twin	16
Full/Queen	30
King	36

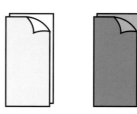

One Block: Place two rectangles of same color wrong sides together.

2. Layer cut on one diagonal.

3. Sort triangles so they are right sides up.

4. Make two different sets.

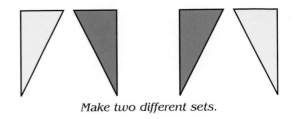

Make two different sets.

Making Flowers

1. Lay out Background triangles with base at bottom. Place Flower triangles on both sides. Make sure all fabrics are turned right side up.

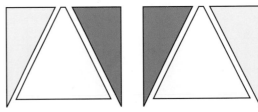

Make two different sets.

2. Set right Flower stacks aside. Flip Background triangle right sides together to Flower in left stack.

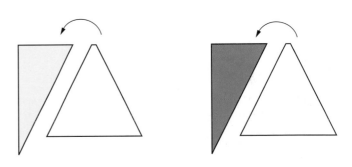

3. Position triangles so Flower extends beyond Background at top, creating a tip at flat top. Flower also extends at bottom.

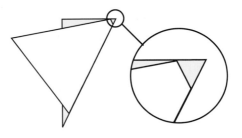

4. Assembly-line sew with an accurate ¼" seam. Use stiletto to guide pieces.

5. Check that seams are still ¼" at points. **Do not trim tips**.

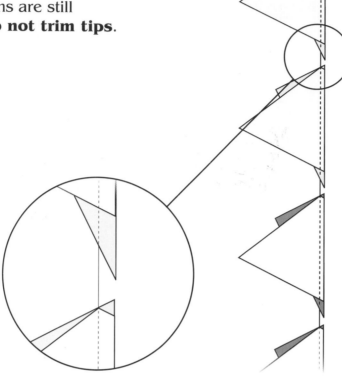

6. Place on pressing mat with Flower on top. Set seams, open, and press toward Flower.

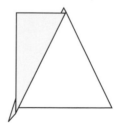
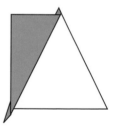

7. Place remaining Flower stacks to right of Backgrounds.

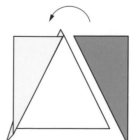
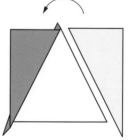

8. Flip right sides together, lining top tip of both pieces together.

9. Assembly-line sew.

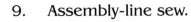
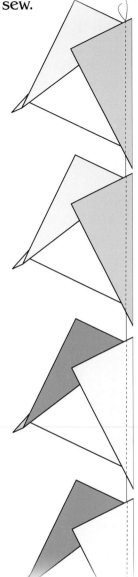

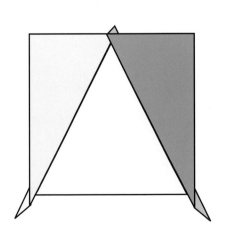

10. Set seams with Flower on top, open, and press toward Flower.

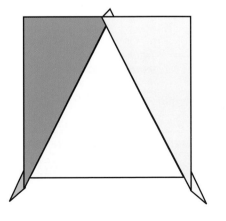

11. Place patch on small cutting mat.

12. Place Triangle in a Square Ruler on patch. Line up ruler's green lines with seams.

13. Square patches to 4½". *Cut around all four sides of ruler, squaring patch to 4½". Turn mat as you cut.*

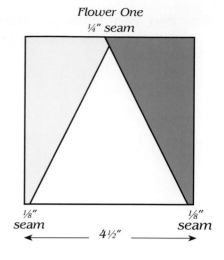

Flower One
¼" seam

¹⁄₈" seam   ¹⁄₈" seam
← 4½" →

	Flower 1	Flower 2
One Block	2	2
Wallhanging	8	8
Lap	24	24
Twin	30	30
Full/Queen	60	60
King	72	72

Making Four-Patches

Sew test set of strips. Width should measure 4½".

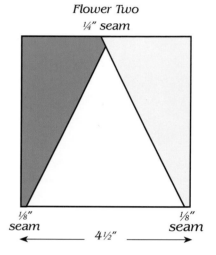

Flower Two
¼" seam

¹⁄₈" seam   ¹⁄₈" seam
← 4½" →

1. Sew 2½" strips right sides together. Use an accurate ¼" seam.

2. Set seams with darkest fabric on top, open, and press toward darkest.

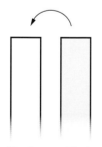

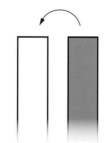

Back-   First
ground   Flower

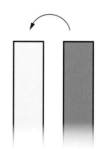

Back-   Second
ground   Flower

First   Second
Flower   Flower

Number of Strips in Each Stack	
One Block	(2) 2½" x 6"
Wallhanging	2 half strips
Lap	6 half strips
Twin	8 half strips
Full/Queen	15 half strips
King	18 half strips

Number of Strips in Each Stack	
One Block	(2) 2½" x 6"
Wallhanging	2 half strips
Lap	6 half strips
Twin	8 half strips
Full/Queen	15 half strips
King	18 half strips

Number of Strips in Each Stack	
One Block	(1) 2½" x 6"
Wallhanging	1 half strip
Lap	3 half strips
Twin	4 half strips
Full/Queen	8 half strips
King	9 half strips

3. **One Block Only:** Cut strip with two Flower fabrics in half into two 3" pieces.

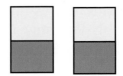

4. Layer strips right sides together on gridded cutting mat. Lock seams. Line up strips with grid.

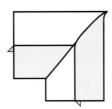 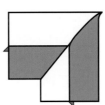

5. Square left end. Cut 2½" pairs from each strip set. Stack on spare ruler and carry to sewing area.

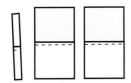 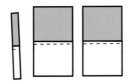

Cut (2) 2½" pairs per block. *Cut (2) 2½" pairs per block.* *Cut (1) 2½" pairs per block.*

Number of Four-Patches of Each Flower	
One Block	2
Wallhanging	8
Lap	24
Twin	30
Full/Queen	60
King	72

Number of Four-Patches of Each Flower	
One Block	2
Wallhanging	8
Lap	24
Twin	30
Full/Queen	60
King	72

Number of Four-Patches of Each Flower	
One Block	1
Wallhanging	4
Lap	12
Twin	15
Full/Queen	30
King	36

6. Matching outside edges and center seam, assembly-line sew. Use stiletto to hold outside edges together and seams flat.

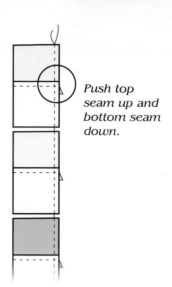

Push top seam up and bottom seam down.

7. Repeat with all pieces for Four-Patches.

8. Open and place wrong side up on pressing mat. Press top vertical seam to right. Press bottom vertical seam to left.

Press top vertical seam to right.

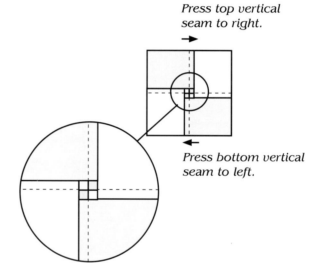

Press bottom vertical seam to left.

9. Flatten center seam, creating a small four-patch. Press seams.

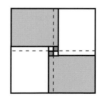
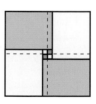

Sewing Block Together

1. Lay out block.

2. Flip middle vertical row to patches on left.

Number of Blocks to Make	
One Block	1
Wallhanging	4
Lap	12
Twin	15
Full/Queen	30
King	36

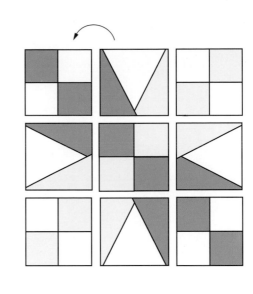

3. Matching outside edges, assembly-line sew.

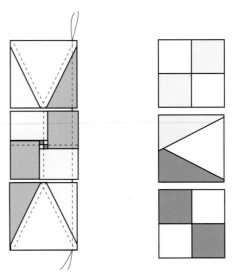

4. Open first two rows.

5. Flip right vertical row to middle row.

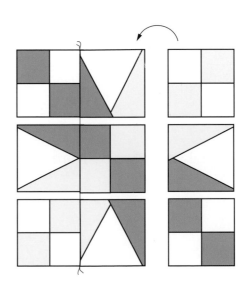

6. Assembly-line sew.

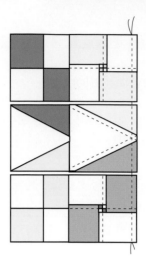

7. Turn block one quarter turn. Flip row on right to middle row. Press seams away from Flower points, and lock together.

8. Assembly-line sew.

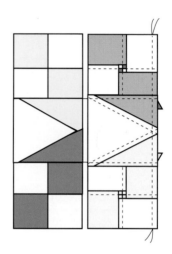

9. Sew last row, pressing seams away from points.

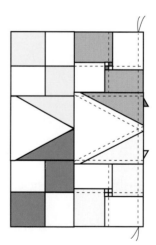

10. Press final seams away from center row.

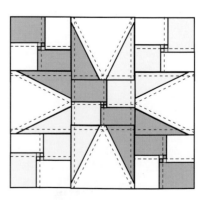

Garden Walk Quilts

Selecting Fabrics

Select one Background fabric that reads solid from a distance. Select one dark for First Flower and one medium for Second Flower that compliment each other. For interest, vary the scales of the two prints.

Purchase additional dark for the Folded Border and Third Border, if needed. Purchase additional medium for Second Border.

Pieced by Teresa Varnes
Quilted by Neta Virgin
55" x 68"

Pieced by Patricia Knoechel
Quilted by Neta Virgin
56" x 71"

Scrappy

Purchase one Background fabric that reads solid from a distance, plus Border fabric. Cut all pieces following chart in your selected size quilt.

Select two colorways from scraps, and divide into coordinating pairs of medium and dark. For each block, cut First Flower and Second Flower pieces following chart on page 181. After blocks are sewn together and laid out, cut Cornerstones from scraps to connect "Walk".

Jewel tones in this quilt stand out on the pale gray background. Multi-toned fabric for the outside border pulled the color scheme together.

Garden Walk Yardage Charts

Finished Block Size 12" square	Wallhanging 2 x 2 = 4 Blocks total 41" x 41"	Lap 3 x 4 = 12 Blocks total 56" x 70"
Background Triangles Four-Patches Lattice First Border	1 yd (2) 5" strips (2) 2½" strips cut in half (4) 2½" strips (4) 2" strips	2⅓ yds (4) 5" strips (6) 2½" strips cut in half (11) 2½" strips (6) 2" strips

First Flower
Flower Points
 	
Four-Patches
Cornerstones
	½ yd
	(1) 6" strip cut into
	    (4) 3" x 6" pairs of rectangles
	(2) 2½" strips cut in half
	(1) 2½" strip cut into
	    (5) 2½" squares
		⅞ yd
		(2) 6" strips cut into
		    (12) 3" x 6" pairs of rectangles
		(5) 2½" strips cut in half
		(1) 2½" strip cut into
		    (10) 2½" squares

Second Flower
Flower Points
 	
Four-Patches
Cornerstones
	½ yd
	(1) 6" strip cut into
	    (4) 3" x 6" pairs of rectangles
	(2) 2½" strips cut in half
	(1) 2½" strip cut into
	    (4) 2½" squares
		⅞ yd
		(2) 6" strips cut into
		    (12) 3" x 6" pairs of rectangles
		(5) 2½" strips cut in half
		(1) 2½" strip cut into
		    (10) 2½" squares

Folded Border	¼ yd (4) 1¼" strips	¼ yd (6) 1¼" strips
Second Border	⅝ yd (4) 4½" strips	1 yd (6) 5½" strips
Third Border		
Binding	½ yd (5) 3" strips	⅔ yd (7) 3" strips
Backing	1½ yds	4½ yds
Batting	48" x 48"	64" x 78"

Twin	Full/Queen	King
3 x 5 = 15 Blocks total **68" x 96"**	**5 x 6 = 30 Blocks total** **96" x 112"**	**6 x 6 = 36 Blocks total** **112" x 112"**
2¾ yds (5) 5" strips (8) 2½" strips cut in half (13) 2½" strips (7) 2" strips	4⅞ yds (9) 5" strips (15) 2½" strips cut in half (24) 2½" strips (9) 2" strips	5¾ yds (11) 5" strips (18) 2½" strips cut in half (28) 2½" strips (10) 2" strips

1⅛ yds
(3) 6" strips cut into
  (16) 3" x 6" pairs of rectangles
(6) 2½" strips cut in half
(1) 2½" strip cut into
  (12) 2½" squares
	2 yds
	(5) 6" strips cut into
	  (30) 3" x 6" pairs of rectangles
	(12) 2½" strips cut in half
	(2) 2½" strips cut into
	  (21) 2½" squares
		2⅓ yds
		(6) 6" strips cut into
		  (36) 3" x 6" pairs of rectangles
		(14) 2½" strips cut in half
		(2) 2½" strips cut into
		  (25) 2½" squares

1⅛ yds
(3) 6" strips cut into
  (16) 3" x 6" pairs of rectangles
(6) 2½" strips cut in half
(1) 2½" strip cut into
  (12) 2½" squares
	2 yds
	(5) 6" strips cut into
	  (30) 3" x 6" pairs of rectangles
	(12) 2½" strips cut in half
	(2) 2½" strips cut into
	  (21) 2½" squares
		2⅓ yds
		(6) 6" strips cut into
		  (36) 3" x 6" pairs of rectangles
		(14) 2½" strips cut in half
		(2) 2½" strips cut into
		  (25) 2½" squares

⅓ yd (7) 1¼" strips	⅜ yd (9) 1¼" strips	⅜ yd (10) 1¼" strips
1 yd (7) 4½" strips	1¼ yds (9) 4½" strips	1⅜ yds (10) 4½" strips
1¾ yds (8) 7" strips	2⅛ yds (10) 7" strips	2¾ yds (11) 8" strips
¾ yd (8) 3" strips	1 yd (11) 3" strips	1⅛ yds (12) 3" strips
6½ yds	9½ yds	10 yds
76" x 104"	104" x 120"	120" x 120"

Laying Out Quilt Top

1. Measure pressed block. Block should be approximately 12½" square.

2. Cut 2½" Lattice strips same length as block.

Number of Lattice	
Wallhanging	12
Lap	31
Twin	38
Full/Queen	71
King	84

3. Place blocks in alternating order.

Blocks Across and Down	
Wallhanging	2 x 2
Lap	3 x 4
Twin	3 x 5
Full/Queen	5 x 6
King	6 x 6

4. Place 2½" Lattice strips and 2½" Cornerstones between blocks. Color of Cornerstone should follow color of "Walk".

5. Assembly-line sew all vertical rows. See pages 203-205.

6. Assembly-line sew remaining rows, pressing seams toward Lattice.

7. Sew Folded Border. See directions on page 98.

8. Turn to *Adding Borders* on page 220.

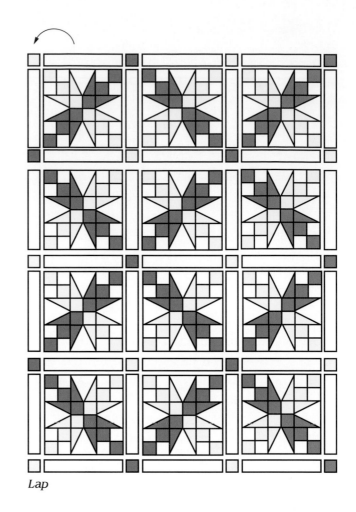

Lap

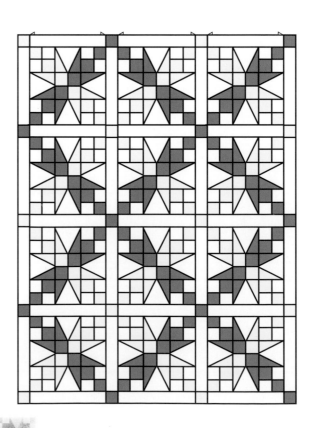

Triangle in a Square Templates

Acrylic Triangle in a Square rulers are available from Quilt in a Day. Cutting with these rulers makes the process easier, and cut pieces are more accurate.

If you do not have these rulers, trace triangle template on template plastic, and cut out. When indicated to use triangle ruler, trace around triangle template with marking pen, and rotary cut on lines with a 6" x 12" Ruler. See page 182.

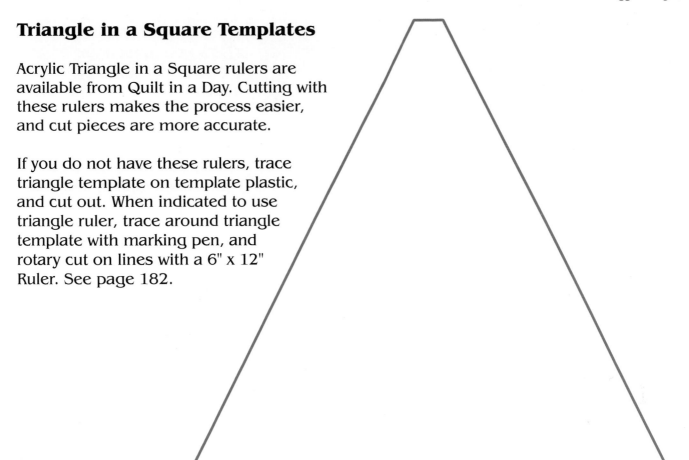

4" Finished Triangle in a Square

Tape 4½" square template plastic on this square, and trace lines with sharp marker.

Tape the 4½" square template to the underneath side of an acrylic 4½" or 6" square ruler.

4½" Square Ruler
Trim four sides.

6" Square Ruler
Place 4½" square template in upper right corner of 6" Ruler. Trim right and top edges. Turn patch, but do not turn ruler. Trim right and top edges.

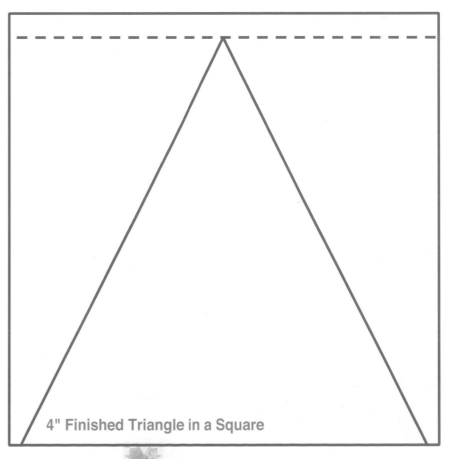

4" Finished Triangle in a Square

*Pieced from antique pieces
by Eleanor Burns
25" x 36"*

As a young woman in Nebraska, Mary Levy may have sent 39 cents to Needlecraft Company in Augusta, Maine for die cut patches of Double Ax. Mary pieced some of the perfect patches together, and then passed her partially sewn quilt to friend Sondra Gordinier, who drove her to guild meetings in later years. Eleanor Burns was the final recipient of the patches, who miraculously sewed them together on the sewing machine, and then hand quilted the top.

If you want to make your own Double Ax, the templates can be found on Block Base by Electric Quilt Company™.

Double Ax Head

Also known as

- *Friendship*
- *Always Friends*
- *Friendship Chain*
- *Double Bit Ax*
- *The Spool*
- *Badge of Friendship*

Samplers One and Two
One 12" Block Finished Size
for each Sampler

Background
(1) 13" square

Nine Different Ax Heads
(9) 5" scrappy print squares

Non-woven Fusible Interfacing
(9) 5" squares

Supplies

❑ Permanent Marking Pen

❑ Ball Point Bodkin

❑ Fat Straw

❑ Wooden Iron

The more the variety, the scrappier the quilt.

Making Nine Ax Heads

1. Find 4¼" circle and ax pattern on large sheet in back of book, and remove.

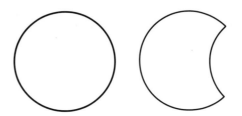

2. Center and trace three 4¼" circles on smooth side of 5" squares lightweight fusible interfacing. Trace six ax heads on smooth side of interfacing.

3. Place bumpy side of interfacing against right side of 5" print squares. Pin.

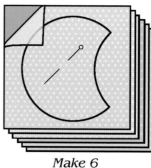
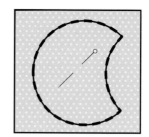

Make 3

Make 6

4. Place metal applique foot on sewing machine. If possible, lighten pressure on presser foot.

5. Sew on drawn line with 20 stitches to the inch. Overlap beginning and ending stitches.

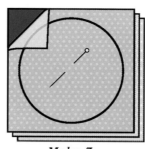
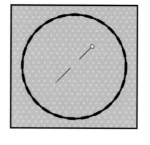

6. Trim circles and ax heads to ⅛" from stitches. Cut a slit in middle of interfacing.

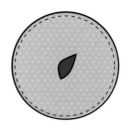

7. Turn pieces right sides out. Run bodkin around inside. Press with wooden iron. Pick out corners of ax heads with stiletto.

8. Press with wooden iron.

 198

Placing Pieces on Background

1. Press Background in fourths.

2. Find pattern in back of book, and remove. Place Background on pattern, lining up folds on Background with center lines on pattern.

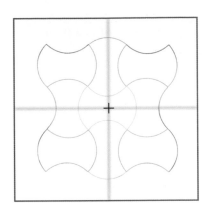

3. Place Background on pressing mat.

4. Place 4¼" circle of fabric in very center of Background.

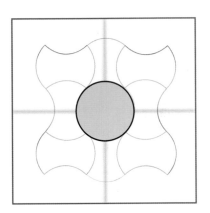

5. Overlap circles on top and bottom of center circle.

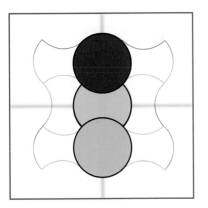

6. Overlap an ax head on each corner.

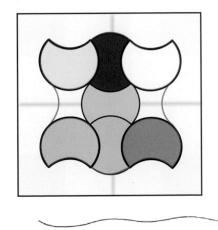

7. Tuck an ax under left and right side of center circle.

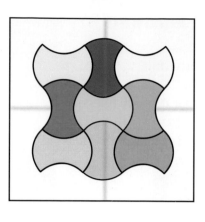

8. Steam press in place from right side with hot iron. Press from wrong side.

9. Blind hem stitch around outside edges with matching or invisible thread.

   Optional: Hand applique in place.

10. Square block to 12½".

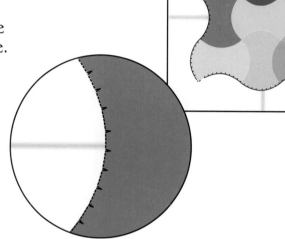

Snickerdoodles

1 cupful shortening
1 1/2 cupfuls white sugar
2 eggs
2 3/4 cupfuls sifted flour
1 teaspoonful baking soda

2 teaspoonfuls cream of tartar
1/2 teaspoonful salt
2 tablespoonfuls white sugar
2 teaspoonfuls ground cinnamon

Preheat your oven to 375 degrees. Lightly grease cookie sheets.

In a large bowl, cream together shortening and sugar. Add one egg at a time and mix after each one. Sift together flour, baking soda, cream of tartar and salt. Stir into shortening and sugar mixture until well blended.

In another smaller bowl, stir together 2 tablespoons of sugar with cinnamon. Roll dough into 1 inch sized balls and roll them in sugar mixture. Place balls 2 inches apart on prepared cookie sheets. Bake for 8-10 minutes in preheated oven. Cookies should be slightly golden around edges. Remove and cool on wire racks.
Makes 3 dozen.

Pieced by Joyce Duarte
Quilted by Neta Virgin
66" x 78"
Zella's Treasures

Made from authentic feed sacks, Joyce's quilt is a delight. Zella, an old family friend, gave the feed sacks to Joyce. The backgrounds on her blocks are different hues of white, cut from various feed sacks. Using scraps left over from the blocks, Joyce pieced her outside border with 2³⁄₄" squares.

Zella Westmoreland See grew up in Twitty, Texas. Her future husband drove from Oklahoma in his custom cruiser to work on Zella's father's farm. What a surprise to meet his bride! Zella's grandmother taught her to quilt when she was just 10 years old, and she enjoyed her hobby to the wonderful old age of 88.

Sewing Blocks Together

Pieced by Patricia Knoechel
Quilted by Judy Jackson
56" x 71"

Yardage to complete quilt is on page 10.

Sampler One Lap Quilt

Checking Sampler One Blocks

1. Check that each block is a consistent size, approximately 12½" square.

2. For blocks larger than consistent size, sliver trim without trimming away any part of the ¼" seam allowance, or resew a wider seam.

    For blocks smaller than consistent size, check seam widths and pressing. If blocks are ¾" smaller than desired size, unsew a few seams and sew again with narrower seam.

3. Do not be concerned if there is a ¼" to ½" variance in block sizes. They can be stretched to size of other blocks.

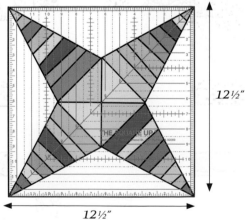

12½"

12½"

Sewing Top Together

1. Lay out blocks three across and four rows down. Blocks can be placed in any order, preferably with different fabrics beside each other.

2. If blocks are less than 12½", trim all Lattice to match consistant block size.

3. Place 2½" Lattice and 2½" Corner-stones between blocks.

4. Flip second vertical row right sides together to first vertical row.

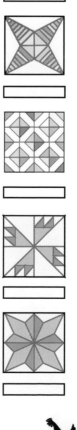

5. Stack from bottom up with top Lattice on top of stack.

6. Assembly-line sew. Stretch or ease each block to fit the Lattice as you sew. Do not clip connecting threads.

7. Open vertical rows one and two.

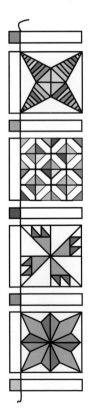

8. Stack third vertical row. Flip pieces in third vertical row right sides together to pieces in second vertical row. Assembly-line sew. Do not clip connecting threads.

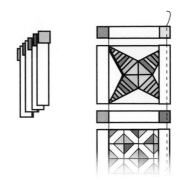

9. Repeat with remaining vertical rows.

10. Lay out quilt top. Check that pieces are in their proper position.

Sewing Horizontal Rows

1. Flip top horizontal row right sides together to second horizontal row. Stretch or ease blocks and Lattice to meet, and sew.

2. At Cornerstones, where pieces are joined by threads, match seams carefully. Push seams toward Lattice for locking seams.

3. Continue sewing all horizontal rows.

4. Press quilt top from the back side, and then from the front.

5. If necessary, straighten outside edges by sliver trimming.

6. Turn to page 220 for *Adding Borders*.

Sampler One Queen Quilt

Yardage to complete quilt is on page 11.

Pieced by Cyndi Reinhardt
Quilted by Laurie McCauley
93" x 111"

With a perfect balance of style and color, Cyndi's quilt has the vintage appeal of the 1930's.

Eggs 10¢ a dozen

Checking Sampler One Blocks

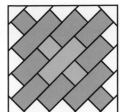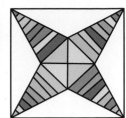

1. Press blocks from wrong side and right side. Trim threads. Measure blocks with 12½" Square Up Ruler. The ideal measurement is 12½".

2. Sort blocks into three stacks:
   - Blocks larger than 12½"
   - Blocks at 12½"
   - Blocks less than 12½"

3. Choose a Frame fabric for each block.

Blocks 12½" and Larger

1. Carefully trim larger blocks to 12½" without removing ¼" seam around outside edges, or resew a wider seam.

2. From each ¼ yd piece, cut a set of Framing strips.
   (2) 2½" strips cut into
       (2) 2½" x 12½" strips
       (2) 2½" x 16½" strips

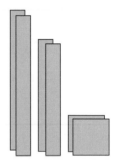

3. From same fabric, cut (2) 4" squares for Cornerstones.

Blocks Measuring Less than 12½"

1. Repress block, and check for wider seams that can be resewn narrower.

2. Cut Framing strips per block.
   (2) 3" strips cut into
       (2) 3" x 12½" strips
       (2) 3" x 17" strips

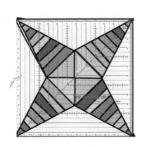

3. From same fabric, cut (2) 4" squares for Cornerstones.

Sewing Frame to Blocks

1. Sew 12½" strips to both sides of block.

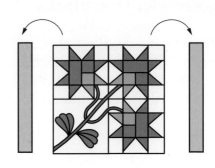

2. Set seams, open, and press seams toward Frame.

3. Trim Frame to size of block.

4. Turn block. Sew remaining strips to both sides of block.

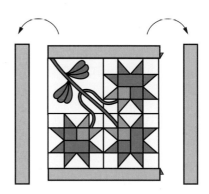

5. Set seams, open, and press seams toward Frame.

6. Square blocks to 16½". Trim equally from four sides.

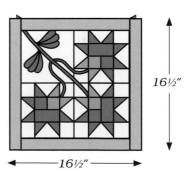

Sewing Top Together

1. Lay out blocks three across and four rows down. Blocks can be placed in any order, preferably with different fabrics beside each other.

2. Place 4" Lattice and 4" Cornerstones between blocks.

3. Assembly-line sew top together following directions on pages 203-205.

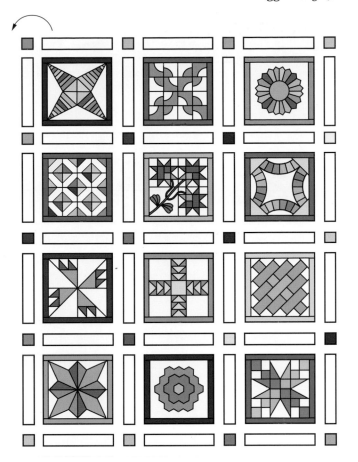

Pieced by Chris Levine
Quilted by Judy Simpson
76" x 96"

Chris neatly framed each block in sage for a clean, crisp looking quilt. Notice her clever arrangement for her Old Maid's Puzzle, so unique! For her wide outside border, Chris selected a cranberry fabric with sage to unite her color scheme.

Sampler Two
Twin Quilt

Pieced by Sue Bouchard
Quilted by Judy Jackson
63" x 84"

Section 1

Section 2

Section 3

Section 4

In addition to the Sampler Two blocks, you need these Background pieces:
(1) 6½" square for Section Two
(1) 3½" x 24½" for Section Three
(1) 3½" x 12½" for Section Four

You need only one Grandmother's Flower Garden block. Use extra block for label on the back.

Sewing Section One Together

1. Sew four Friendship blocks together. Press just sewn seams to right.

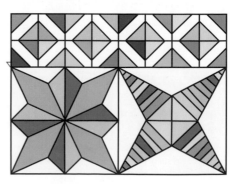

2. Sew Rocky Road and Turkey Tracks blocks together, or any two 12½" blocks. Press seam to the left.

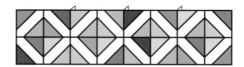

3. Sew Friendship blocks and two 12½" blocks together. Press just sewn seam toward Friendship blocks.

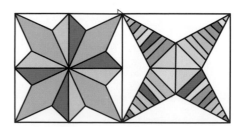

4. Sew two 9½" Christian Cross blocks together. Press seam toward top Christian Cross.

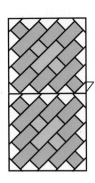

5. Lay out all blocks in Section One and sew together.

6. Press just sewn seams from center to outside edges.

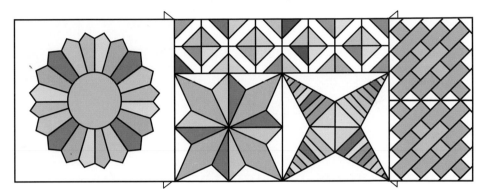

Sewing Section Two Together

1. Sew three Friendship blocks together with 6½" Background square. Press just sewn seams toward Background square.

2. Sew Friendship row to Old Maid's Puzzle blocks. Press just sewn seam toward Friendship row.

3. Sew Grandmother's Flower Garden and Rosebuds together. Press vertical seam toward Grandmother's Flower Garden.

4. Sew to Old Maid's Puzzle block.

5. Press seam toward top.

Sewing Section Three Together

1. Sew two 9½" Christian Cross blocks together. Press seam toward top.

2. Sew Christian Cross together with Road to California.

3. Press seam toward Road to California.

4. Sew Peony block to 3½" x 24½" Background strip.

5. Press just sewn seam toward Background strip.

6. Sew Road to California/Christian Cross block to Peony.

7. Press seam toward Peony.

Sewing Sections Two and Three Together

1. Place Section Three right sides together to Section Two.

2. Match and pin seams.

3. Sew together.

4. Press just sewn seam toward Section Three.

Sewing Four Sections Together

1. Sew Section One to Sections Two/Three, matching and pinning seams together.

2. Press seam toward Section Two/Three.

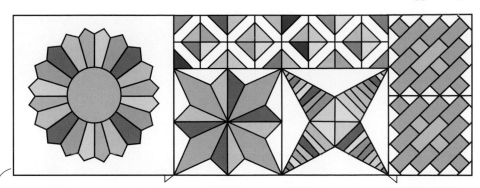

3. Sew three Double Wedding Ring blocks together. Press just sewn seams toward center block.

4. Sew Garden Walk to 3½" x 12½" Background strip and three Double Wedding Ring blocks.

5. Press just sewn seams toward Background strip.

6. Sew Section Four to Sections One/ Two/Three. Press just sewn seams away from Section Two/Three.

7. Turn to *Adding Borders*, page 220.

Sampler Two Queen Quilt

Pieced by Eleanor Burns
Quilted by Carol Selepec
78" x 90"

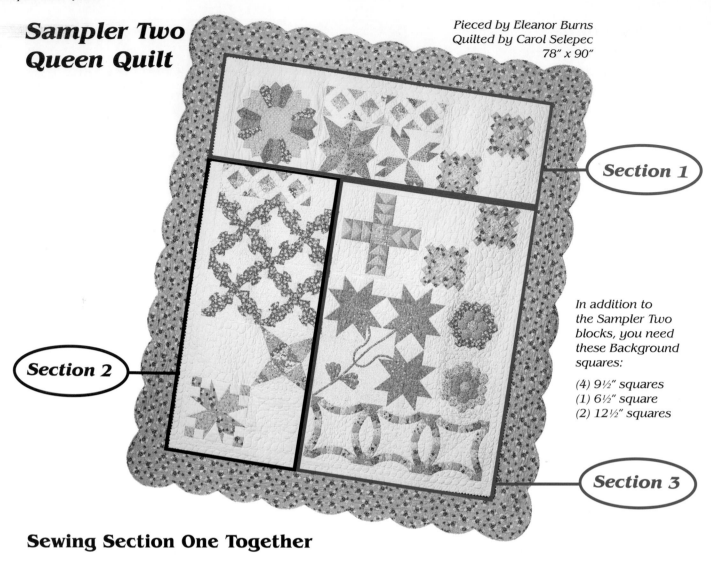

Section 1

Section 2

Section 3

In addition to the Sampler Two blocks, you need these Background squares:

(4) 9½" squares
(1) 6½" square
(2) 12½" squares

Sewing Section One Together

1. Sew four Friendship blocks together. Press just sewn seams to right.

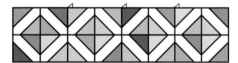

2. Sew Rocky Road and Turkey Tracks blocks together, or any two 12½" blocks. Press seam to the left.

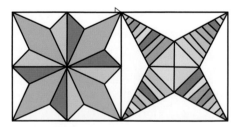

3. Sew Friendship blocks and two 12½" blocks together. Press just sewn seam toward Friendship blocks.

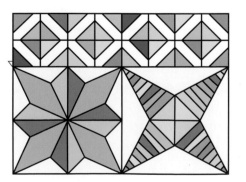

4. Sew two 9½"
    Christian Cross
    blocks together
    with two 9½"
    Background
    squares. Press
    seams toward
    Background
    squares.

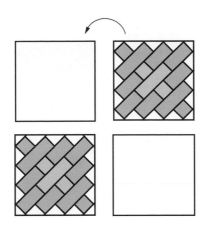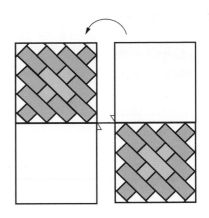

5. Press just sewn
    seams to one side.

6. Lay out
    all blocks
    in Section
    One and
    sew
    together.

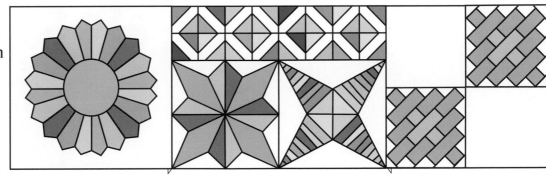

7. Press
    just sewn
    seams from center to outside edges.

Sewing Section Two Together

1. Sew three Friendship blocks together
    with 6½" Background square. Press
    just sewn seams toward Background
    square.

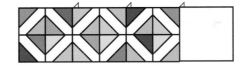

2. Sew Friendship row to Old Maid's
    Puzzle blocks. Press just sewn seam
    toward Friendship row.

3. Sew Rosebuds and Garden Walk together with two 12½" Background squares. Press vertical seam toward Background.

4. Sew remaining row. Press just sewn seam to one side.

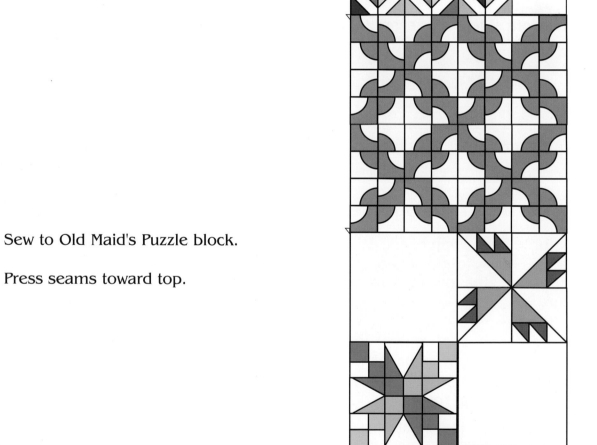

5. Sew to Old Maid's Puzzle block.

6. Press seams toward top.

Sewing Section Three Together

1. Sew two 9½" Christian Cross blocks together with two 9½" Background squares. Press seams toward Background.

2. Sew remaining row. Press just sewn seam to one side.

3. Sew Christian Cross together with Road to California.

4. Press seam toward Road to California.

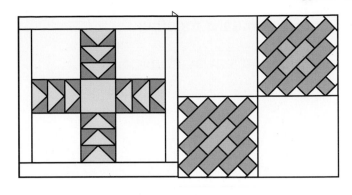

5. Sew two Grandmother's Flower Garden blocks together.

6. From right side, press seam to left.

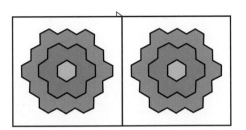

7. Sew Grandmother's Flower Garden to Peony block.

8. Press just sewn seam toward Grandmother's Flower Garden.

9. Sew three Double Wedding Ring blocks together.

10. Press just sewn seams toward center block.

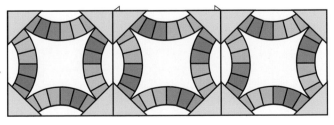

11. Sew three units together.

12. Press seams away from center.

Sewing Three Sections Together

1. Place Section Three right sides together to Section Two.

2. Match and pin seams together.

3. Sew together.

4. Press just sewn seam toward Section Three.

218

5. Sew Section One to Sections Two/Three, matching and pinning seams together.

6. Press seam toward Section Two/Three.

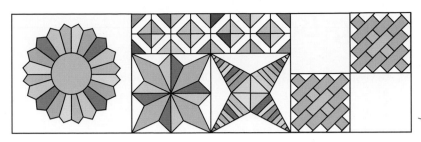

Pieced and Quilted by Lois Bretzlaff
92" x 104"

Lois chose jewel tones on her Bali Batik background fabric to create the illusion of stained glass. She used three borders to frame her quilt and made it large enough for her queen size bed.

Adding Borders

There are three Border selections to choose from:
- Straight Border
- Scalloped Border
- Rainbow Border

You can custom size your quilt by changing Borders to any width. However, this may affect Backing and Batting yardages.

Adding Straight Borders

1. Cut Border strips according to your Yardage Chart.

2. Trim selvages.

3. Assembly-line sew into long pieces.

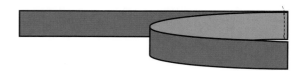

Lay first strip right side up. Lay second strip right sides to it. Backstitch, stitch, and backstitch again.

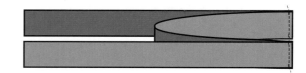

4. Cut Border pieces the average length of both sides.

5. Pin to sides. Sew from quilt side with Border on the bottom, so seams are sewn in direction they were pressed.

6. Fold out and press seams toward Border.

7. Measure the width and cut Border pieces for top and bottom. Pin and sew.

8. Press seams toward Border.

9. Turn to page 224 for *Layering Your Quilt.*

Marking Scalloped Border

Strips for scallops are cut 15" wide so they cover sides of queen size top mattress. They can be cut any width you choose to fit your bed. You may even choose to leave off the top Border strip.

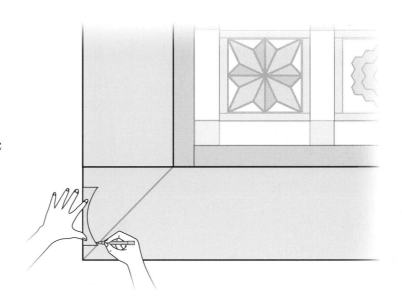

1. Find scallop template in back of book and remove.

2. Mark diagonal lines with hera™ marker on corners.

3. Place corner of scallop template on diagonal line. Line up edge of scallop template with raw edge of Border. Trace with disappearing pen.

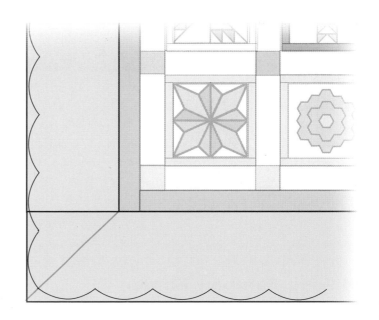

4. Mark scallops from two ends toward middle. Make adjustment in very center scallop to fit. You may need to elongate center scallops or shorten.

5. Turn to page 224 for *Layering Your Quilt*.

6. After quilt is quilted, sew on drawn scallop line and trim ⅛" away.

7. *Bias Binding* begins on page 231.

Rainbow Border

This is the perfect 4½" wide scrappy Border to finish off a quilt when you have used all your large pieces of fabric in the blocks, and can't find a suitable substitute for a Border.

Sampler One Lap

Fifteen Different Fabrics
(2) 2½" half strips from each
or a total of (30) 2½" half strips

All Other Quilts

Fifteen Different Fabrics
(3) 2½" half strips from each
or a total of (45) 2½" half strips

Corners

(4) 5" squares

Egg Money Sampler One
Pieced by Sue Bouchard
Quilted by Judy Jackson
60" x 75"

Calculate Your Own Rainbow Border

To make a 5" x 120" Border:

- Cut (15) 2½" half strips from (15) different fabrics.
- Sew together lengthwise.
- Cut into (4) 5" sections.
- Sew together end to end.

Making Rainbow Border

1. Cut 2½" half strips of fabric from your left-overs. If necessary, piece scraps of same color to approximately 21" in length.

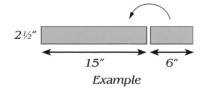

2½"

15"   6"

Example

2. Sew fifteen 2½" strips together lengthwise with ¼" seam.

Sampler One Lap	Two sets
Sampler One Queen	Three sets
Sampler Two Twin	Three sets
Sampler Two Queen	Three sets

3. Press seams in one direction.

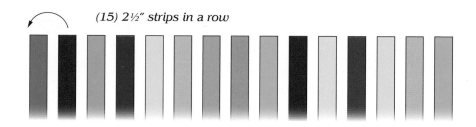

(15) 2½" strips in a row

4. Fold in half lengthwise. Square left edge. Cut each set into four 5" sections.

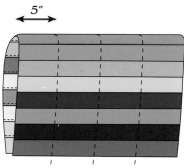

5"

Cut into (4) 5" sections.

5. Piece together end to end into two lengths and two widths same measurement as quilt top. Trim off extra.

6. Pin and sew Border to sides. Press seams away from Border.

7. Sew 5" Corners to both ends of top and bottom. Press seams toward Corners.

8. Sew Border to top and bottom. Press seams away from Border.

9. Turn to page 224 for *Layering Your Quilt.*

Layering Your Quilt

1. If necessary, piece Backing.

2. Spread out Backing on a large table or floor area, right side down. Clamp fabric to edge of table with quilt clips, or tape Backing to floor. Do not stretch Backing.

3. Layer Batting on Backing and pat flat.

4. With quilt right side up, center on Backing and Batting. Smooth until all layers are flat. Clamp or tape outside edges.

Safety Pinning

1. Place pin covers on 1" safety pins. Safety pin through all layers three to five inches apart. Pin away from where you plan to quilt.

2. Catch tip of pin in grooves on pinning tool, and close pins.

3. Use pinning tool to open pins when removing them. Store pins opened.

Machine Quilting

Quilting "In the Ditch"
with Walking Foot

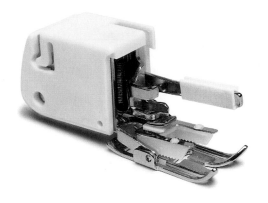

1. Thread your machine with matching,
    contrasting, or invisible thread. If you use
    invisible thread, loosen your top tension.
    Match bobbin thread to Backing.

2. Attach walking foot, and lengthen
    stitch to 8 to 10 stitches per inch
    or 3.0 on computerized machines.

3. Tightly roll quilt from one long side to
    center. Place hands on quilt in triangular
    shape, and spread seams open. "Stitch in
    the ditch" along seam lines, and anchor
    blocks and border.

4. Roll quilt in opposite direction, and stitch
    in ditch along seam lines.

Quilting Blocks with Darning Foot

1. Attach darning foot to sewing machine. Drop feed dogs or cover feed dogs with a plate. No stitch length is required as you control the length by your sewing speed. Use a fine needle and invisible or regular thread in the top and regular thread to match the Backing in the bobbin. Loosen top tension if using invisible thread. Use needle down position.

The advantage of using a darning foot to quilt is that you don't need to constantly pivot and turn a large heavy quilt as you do with a walking foot.

2. Plan how to stitch, covering as many seams continuously as possible.

3. Place hands flat on block. Bring bobbin thread up on seam line.

4. Lock stitch and clip thread tails. Free motion stitch in the ditch around block. Keep top of block at top. Sew sideways and back and forth without turning quilt.

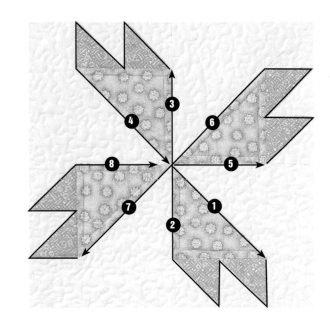

5. If desired, quilt ¼" away from seams.

6. Fill in Background area by stitching a few stitches in one direction. Curve around and stitch back toward the beginning, making a loop. Continue making loops until Background area is filled. This technique is called "stippling."

7. Lock stitches and cut threads.

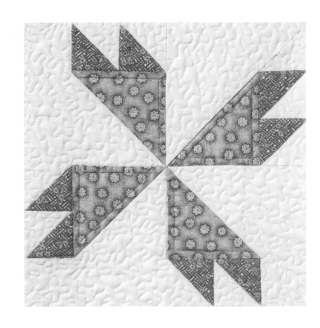

226

Marking for Free Motion Quilting

1. Select an appropriate stencil.

2. Center on area to be quilted, and trace lines with disappearing marker. An alternative method is lightly spraying fabric with water, and dusting talc powder into lines of stencil.

3. Attach darning foot to sewing machine. Drop feed dogs or cover feed dogs with a plate. No stitch length is required as you control the length. Use a fine needle and invisible or regular thread in the top and regular thread to match the Backing in the bobbin. Loosen top tension if using invisible thread.

4. Place hands flat on sides of marking. Bring bobbin thread up on line. Lock stitch and clip thread tails.

5. Free motion stitch around design. Lock stitches and cut threads.

Binding
Making Straight Binding

1. Place walking foot attachment on sewing machine and regular thread on top and in bobbin to match Binding.

2. Square off selvage edges, and sew 3" Binding strips together lengthwise. Fold and press in half with wrong sides together.

3. Line up raw edges of folded Binding with raw edges of quilt in middle of one side. Begin stitching 4" from end of Binding. Sew with 10 stitches per inch, or 3.0 to 3.5. Sew ⅜" from edge, or width of walking foot.

4. At corner, stop stitching ⅜" in from edge with needle in fabric. Raise presser foot and turn quilt toward corner.

5. Put foot back down. Stitch diagonally off edge of Binding.

6. Raise foot, and pull quilt forward slightly. Turn quilt to next side.

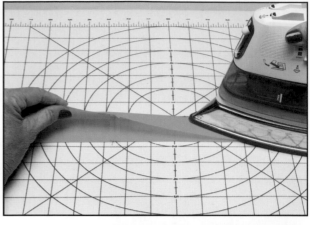

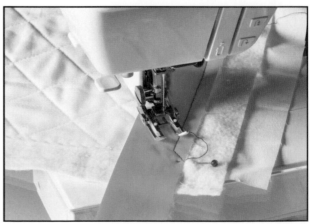
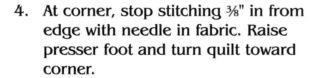

7. Fold Binding strip straight up on diagonal. Fingerpress diagonal fold.

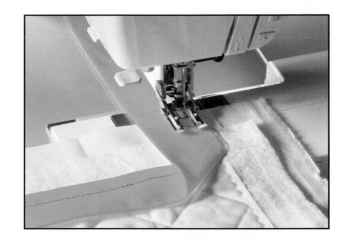

8. Fold Binding strip straight down with diagonal fold underneath. Line up top of fold with raw edge of Binding underneath.

9. Begin sewing from edge.

10. Continue stitching and mitering corners around outside of quilt.

11. Stop stitching 4" from where ends will overlap.

12. Line up two ends of Binding. Trim excess with ½" overlap.

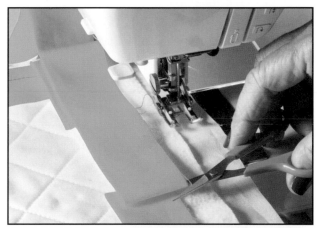

13. Open out folded ends and pin right sides together. Sew a ¼" seam.

14. Continue stitching Binding in place.

15. Trim Batting and Backing up to ⅛" from raw edges of Binding.

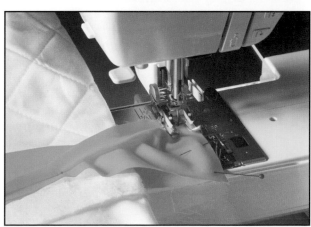

16. Fold back Binding.

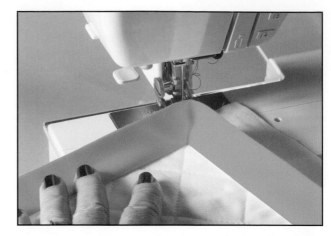

17. Pull Binding to back side of quilt. Pin in place so that folded edge on Binding covers stitching line. Tuck in excess fabric at each miter on diagonal.

18. From right side, "stitch in the ditch" using invisible thread on front side, and bobbin thread to match Binding on back side. Catch folded edge of Binding on the back side with stitching.

   Optional: Hand stitch Binding in place.

19. Hand stitch miter.

20. Sew identification label on Back.

Use extra block. Sign name, date, city, state, and any other pertinent information

on Background space with permanent marking pen, or machine lettering. Turn raw edges under ¼". Pin to back side of quilt, and hand stitch in place around outside edge.

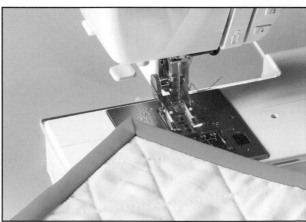

Making Bias Binding for Scalloped Borders

1. Cut Binding fabric into 16" selvage to selvage strips.

2. Line up 45° line on 6" x 24" ruler with left edge of 16" strip.

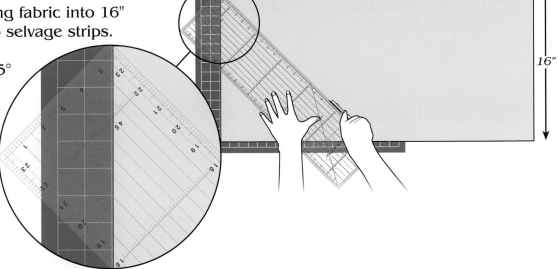

3. Cut on diagonal. Fabric from triangle to left of ruler can be cut into bias strips as well.

4. Move ruler over 2" from diagonal cut. Cut again.

5. Cut 16" strip into 2" bias strips.

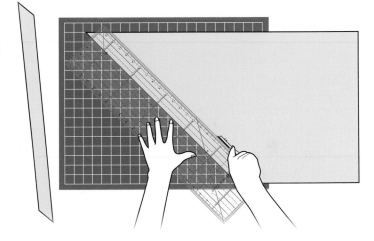

6. Piece bias strips together on angle to outside measurements of your quilt.

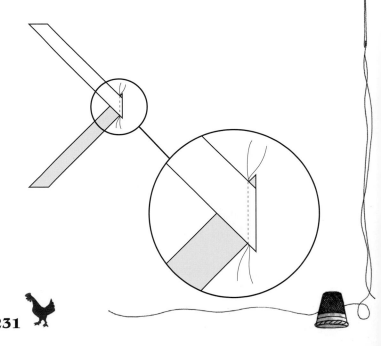

7. Press diagonal seams open.

8. Press bias strip in half lengthwise wrong sides together.

9. Line up raw edge of Binding with marked scallop line. Leave 3" of Binding loose. Begin stitching scant ¼" seam in middle of scallop.

10. Stitch to point between two scallops. Stop with needle in fabric.

11. Raise presser foot, pivot and continue stitching around quilt, easing binding around curves.

12. Stop stitching 4" from where ends will overlap.

13. Line up the two ends of Binding. Trim the excess with a ½" overlap.

14. Open up folded ends and pin right sides together. Sew a ¼" seam.

15. Continue stitching Binding in place.

16. Trim quilt top even with Binding. Clip between scallops to seam.

17. Turn Binding to back side. Pull folded edge over stitching line. Inside corners will automatically fold in place. Hand stitch folded edge.

18. See label on page 230.

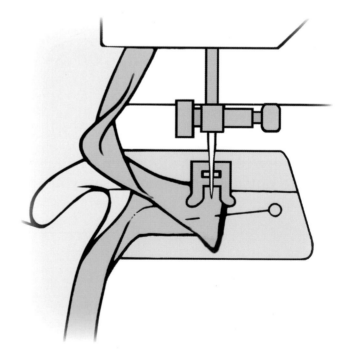

Acknowledgements

A grateful thank you to these dedicated women who shared their quilts, family heirlooms, and talents, including all my students in 2004 Block Party!

Penny Anthony	Jeffie Ehn	Laurie McCauley	Judi Sample
Fran Bisner	Sondra Gordinier	Millie Norville	Carol Selepec
Sue Bouchard	Yvette Hallbick	Elizabeth Pfeiffer	Judy Simpson
Lois Bretzlaff	Cleatis Hofer	Amie Potter	Jeane Stellmack
Jeanne Crone	Judy Jackson	Pamela Rabehl	Sandy Thompson
Anne Dease	Patricia Knoechel	Cyndi Reinhardt	Teresa Varnes
Mary Devendorf	Chris Levine	Brenda Richmond	Neta Virgin
Joyce Duarte	Snookie Marier	Karen Ryan	Brenda Witt
Cora Eaton	Margaret Massey	Aiko Rogers	

Student Gallery

Hilary Olmstead & Lynn Cantrell

Tea Room

Rose McCoy & Jeanette Hallbick

In 2004, Eleanor Burns taught a 1930's monthly Block Party to 80 students. All year, they had a great time sharing their families' antique quilts, aprons, and old time stories. Eleanor showed them how to assemble Depression era blocks with quick methods, yet blocks maintained a traditional look. The class celebrated their accomplishments and friendship with a tea party. Some students dressed for the time period! The highlight of the event was the sharing of their finished Egg Money quilts. Celebrate with them, and enjoy looking at their creativity.

Eleanor Burns

Terri Eckhardt, Lois Bretzlaff & Sharon Kleven

Brenda Richmond

My First Attempt 54" x 69"
Pieced and Quilted by Elizabeth Pfeiffer

In her fresh summery quilt, Elizabeth arranged Old Maid's Puzzle in the Dirty Windows design. Using scraps of fabric from her blocks, she made a folded border to frame her quilt, and Friendship blocks for cornerstones.

Egg Money Sampler One 50" x 64"
Pieced and Tied by Fran Bisner

Fran used crisp white to make her soft shades of red, blue, yellow and green really stand out. Her red lattice and paisley border tie her color scheme together perfectly.

Depression Era Paisley 62" x 78"
Pieced by Cora Eaton
Quilted by Jeffie Ehn

Cora framed her blocks with a rich, red fabric that has a linen look to it. Her quilt features sage green and red paisley fabric with large, overall stippling.

Splash of Batik 63" x 75"
Pieced and Quilted by Karen Ryan

Beautiful blues and lavenders, with a touch of gold for good measure, give Karen's quilt a magical look. She rearranged her "Old Maid's Puzzle" squares into an original design and repeated puzzle pieces in her cornerstones.

Momma's Apron 56" x 70"
Pieced by Pamela Rabehl
Quilted by Joyce Duarte

Pamela machine blanket stitched in black thread around Grandmother's Flower Garden, Dresden Plate, and Double Wedding Ring, just like the 1930's. Her Christian Cross finished a little too large so her attitude was "Not to worry, just trim it to size!"

Egg Money Sampler Two 72" x 85"
Pieced by Aiko Rogers
Quilted by Neta Virgin

What a lovely sampler quilt! Aiko's Old Maid's Puzze is especially striking pieced with just one fabric, her Peony blooms bright, and those old Turkey Tracks are just ready for trotting.

Christmas Cheer 51" x 64"
Pieced and Quilted by Millie Norville

Using traditional holiday colors, Millie created a quilt with great balance of color. Her Peony block has four flowers without stems for a star-like pattern. When her "Friendship" block finished slightly smaller than expected, Millie simply added a narrow border!

The Talk of the Prairie 63" x 78"
Pieced and Quilted by Yvette Hallbick

Yvette chose rich prairie colors for her quilt, and used multiple fabrics for each block. Notice her Peony, Garden Walk, and Christian Cross. Her unique arrangement of Old Maid's Puzzle adds interest. To unite her color palette, Yvette found the perfect outside border fabric.

All Nighter 78" x 90"
Pieced and Quilted by Penny Anthony

Penny added the fourth flower to her Peony, without stems, for a quick, lovely arrangement. The quilt is so named because Penny worked all night to get it to the photographer in time!

Pointless Wonder 50" x 63"
Pieced and Quilted by Snookie Marier

Using the Double Wedding Ring blocks as an entire row catches your eye in Snookie's attractive quilt. When she was done with her quilt, Snookie stood back and exclaimed, "What happened to my points!

Index

Order Information

Quilt in a Day books offer a wide range of techniques and are directed toward a variety of skill levels. If you do not have a quilt shop in your area, you may write or call for a complete catalog and current price list of all books and patterns published by Quilt in a Day®, Inc.

Quilt in a Day®, Inc. • 1955 Diamond Street • San Marcos, CA 92078
1 800 777-4852 • Fax: (760) 591-4424 • www.quiltinaday.com

I Remember Grandma
Pieced by Eleanor Burns
Quilted by Judy Jackson
78" x 90"

$\mathcal{R}$eminiscing of grandma's kitchen and days gone by, Eleanor chose to use "Kaye's Kitchen," a nostalgic fabric line from Benartex, for her cheerful Sampler Two. The jumbo yellow rickrack embellishes the quilt while the black scalloped border compliments the bright red frame. Eleanor skillfully used bits of twelve fabrics to give her quilt an old fashioned scrappy look.